DAY OF THE DEAD TIRED

AN ADULT COLORING BOOK TO HELP RELIEVE THE STRESS OF THE BAD DAY YOU'RE HAVING

This is not for the faint of heart coloring book. Some images are quite intricate and will require 100% of your attention. ENJOY!

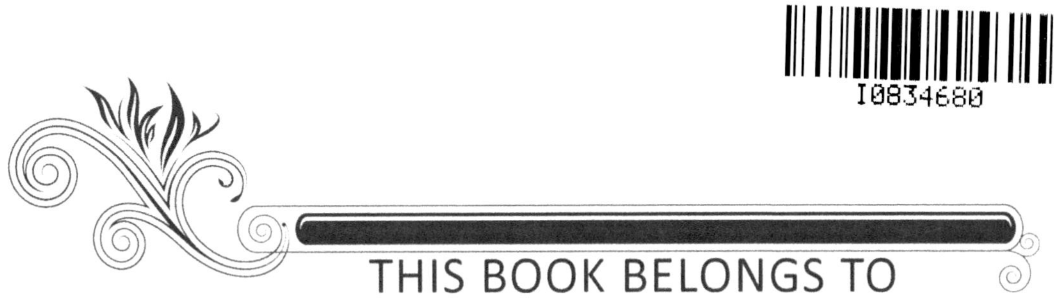

ISBN: 978-1-63415-548-9
Cover Art Designed by Dawné Dominique

Published by DusktilDawn Publications
CANADA

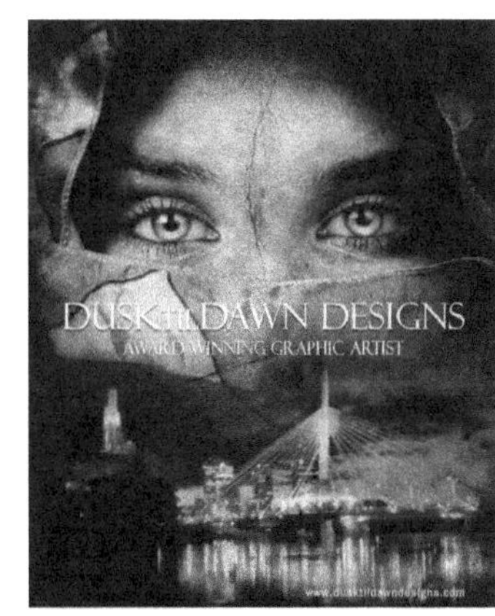

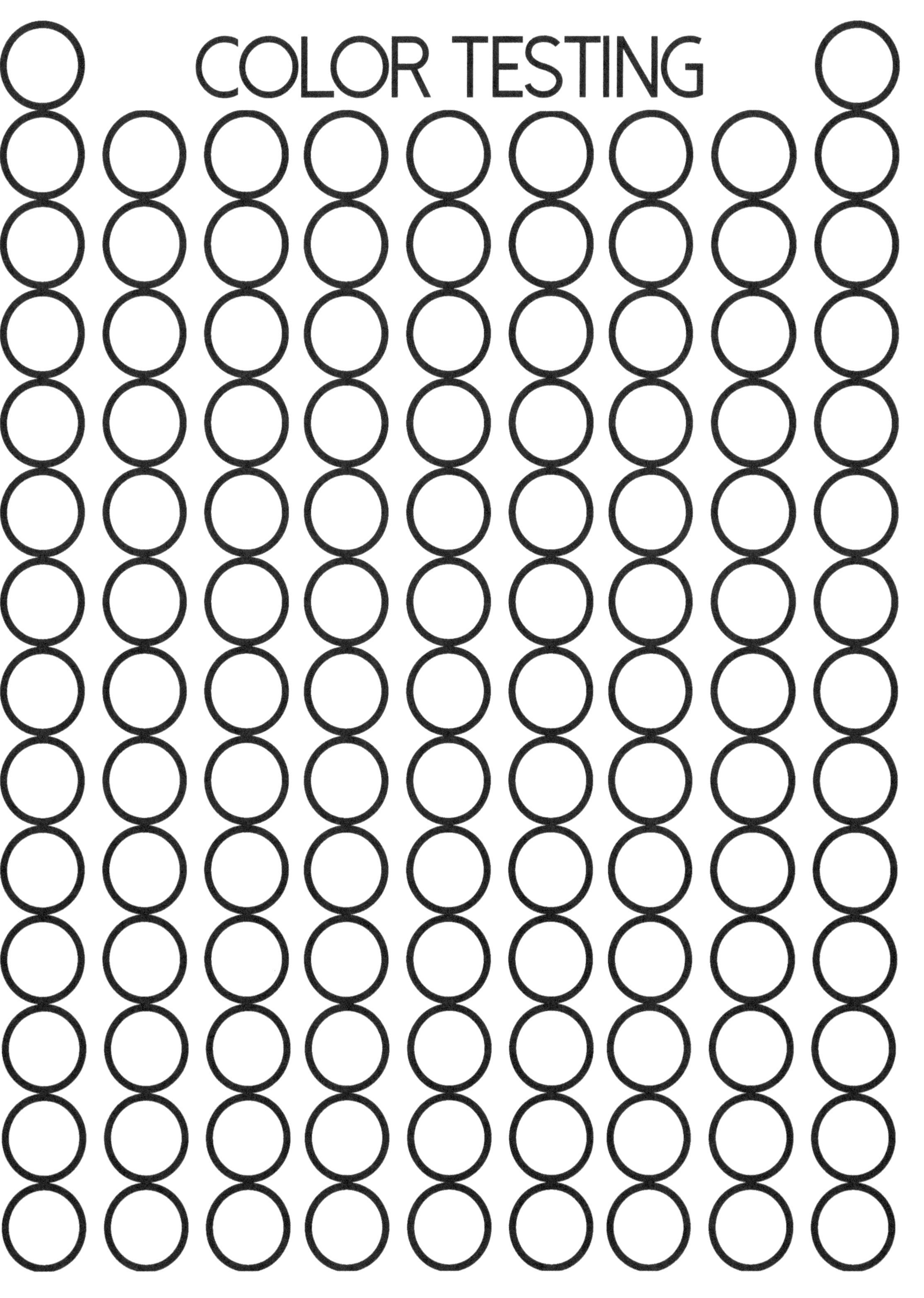
COLOR TESTING

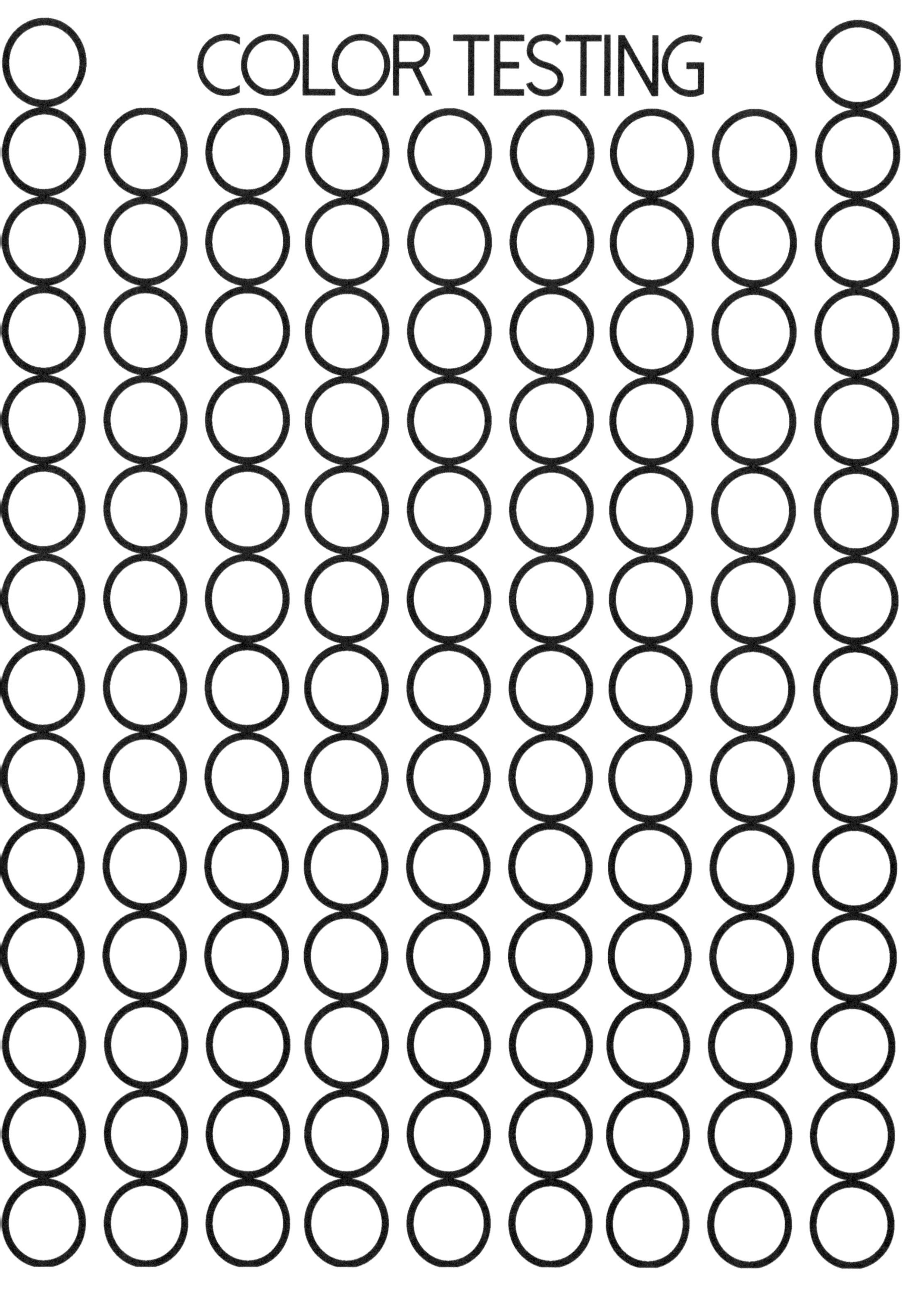
COLOR TESTING

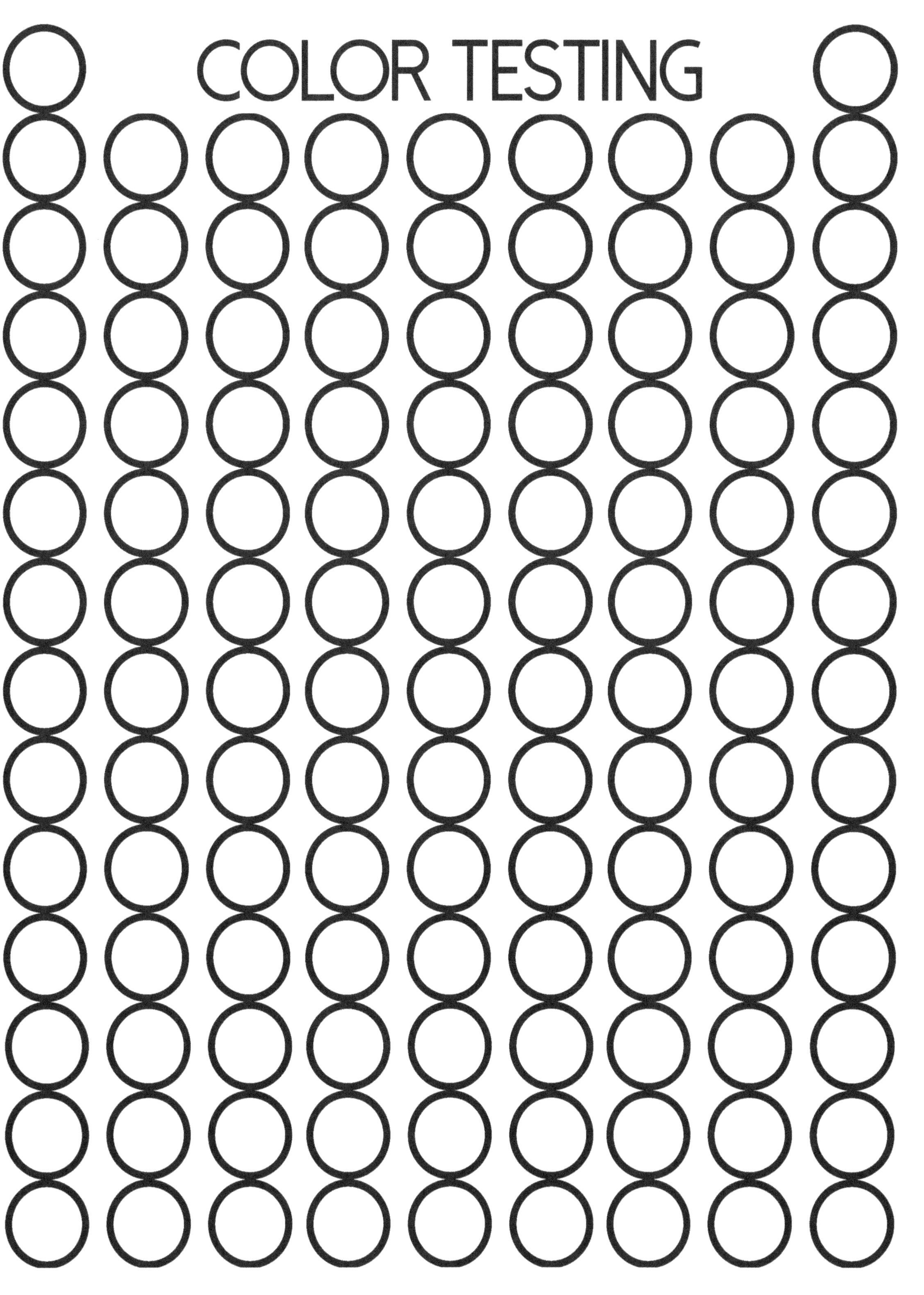
COLOR TESTING

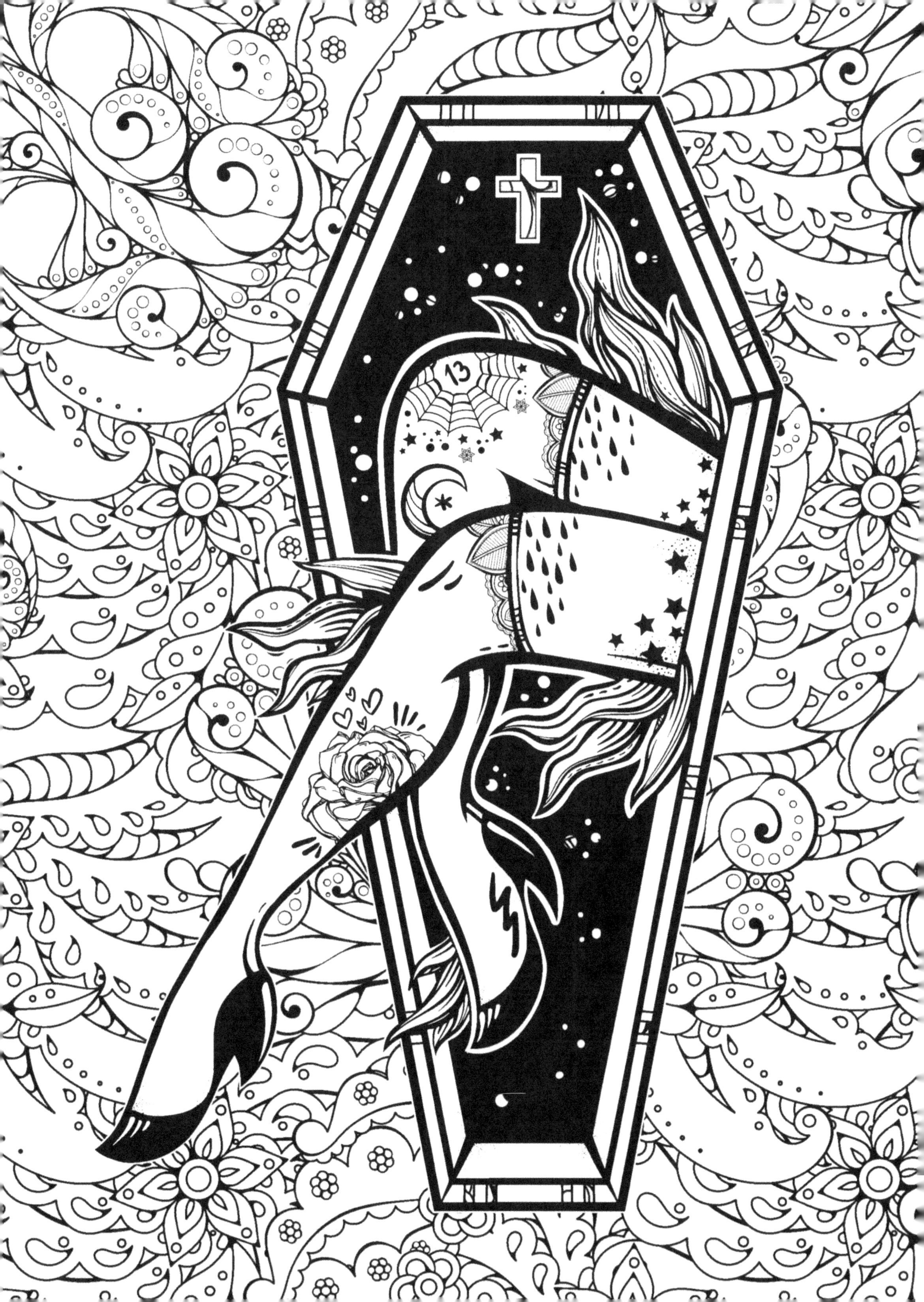

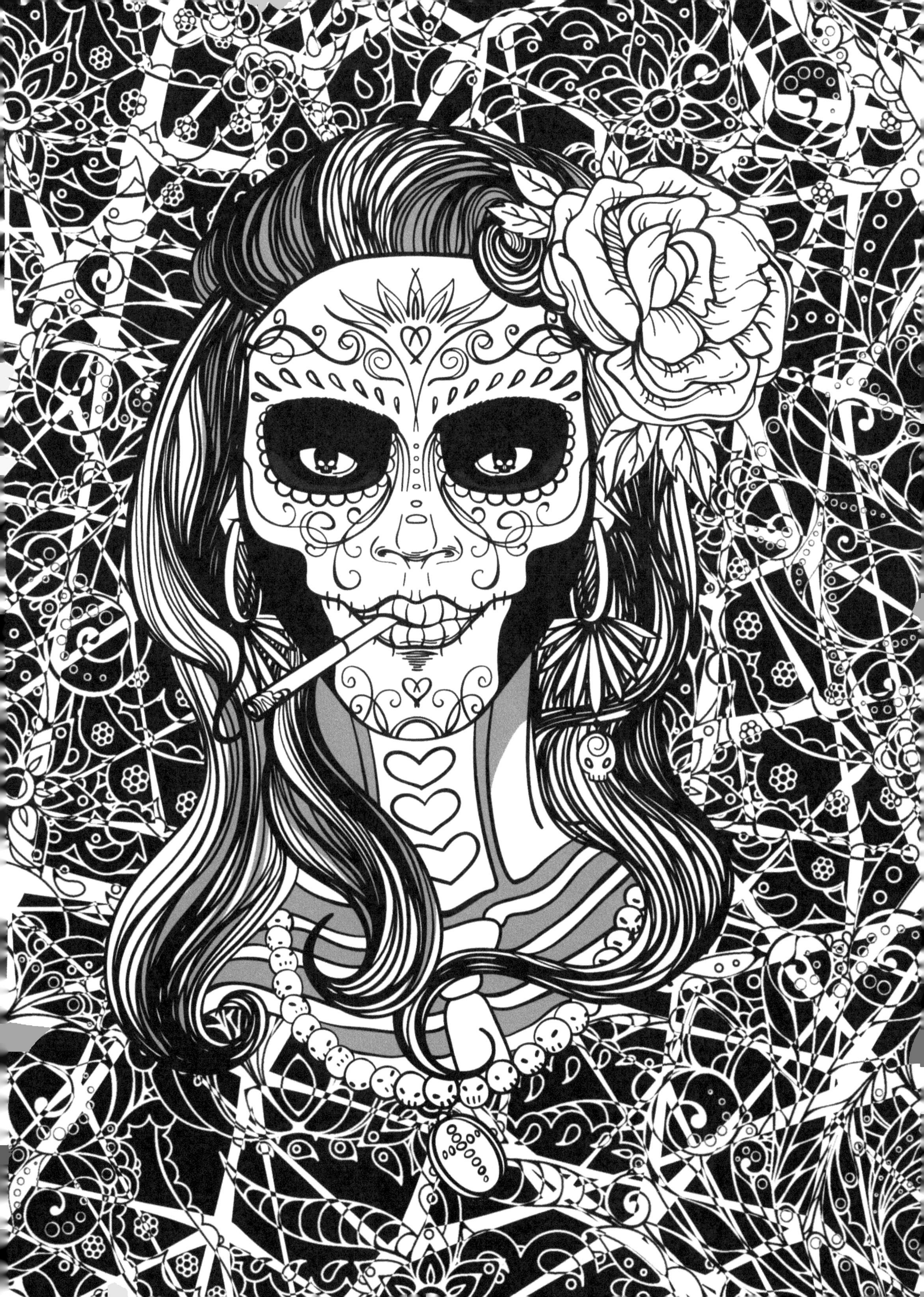

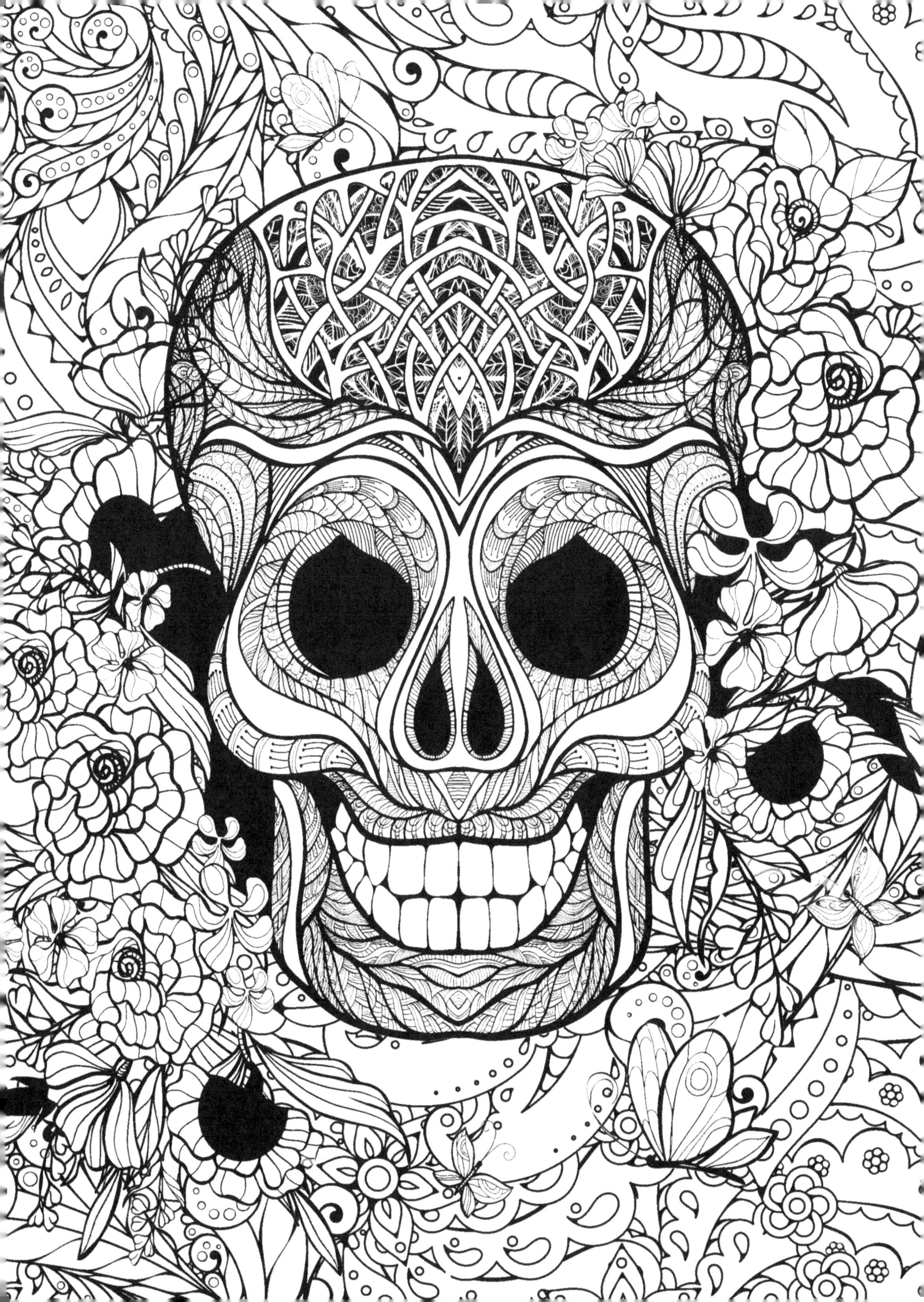

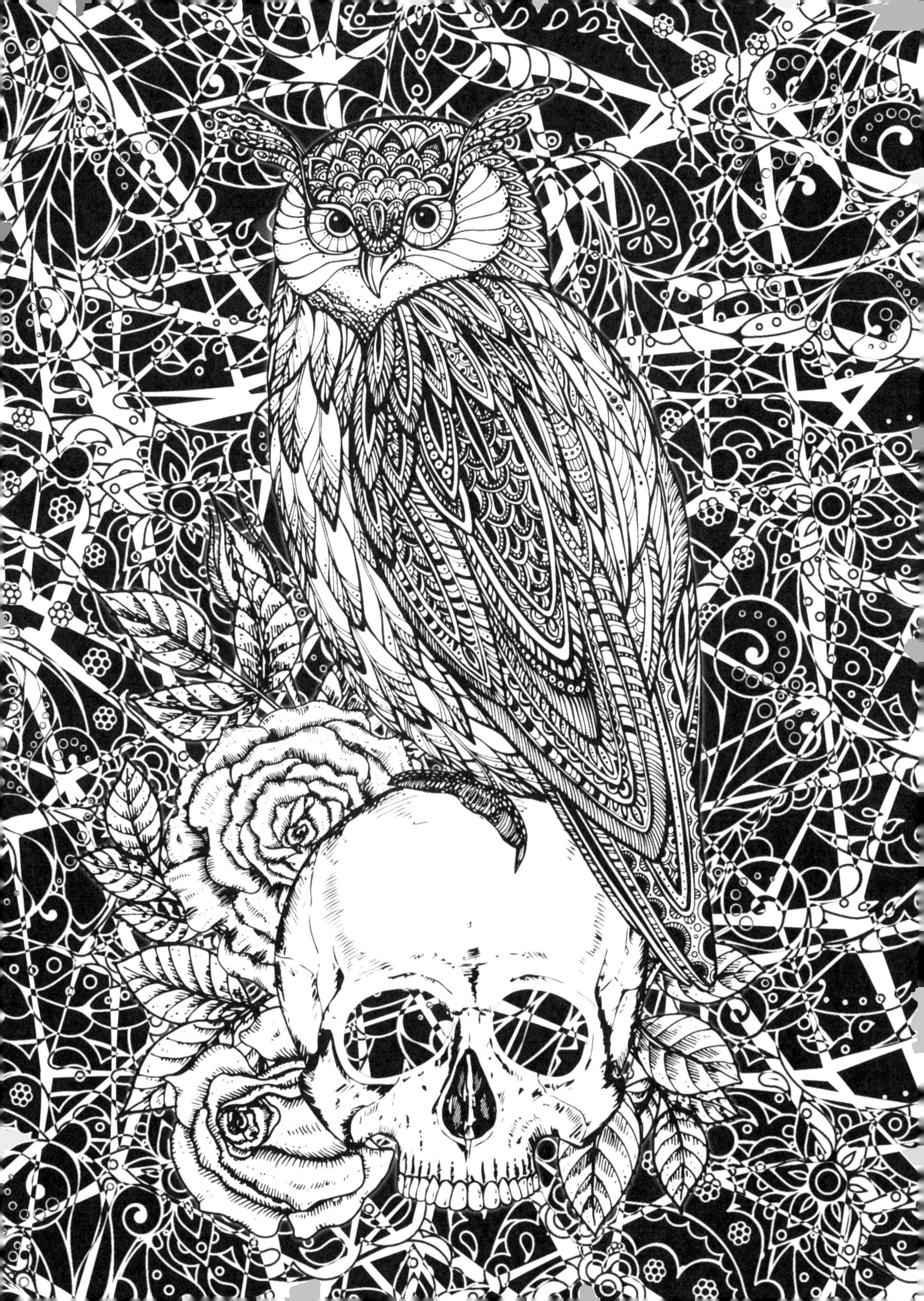

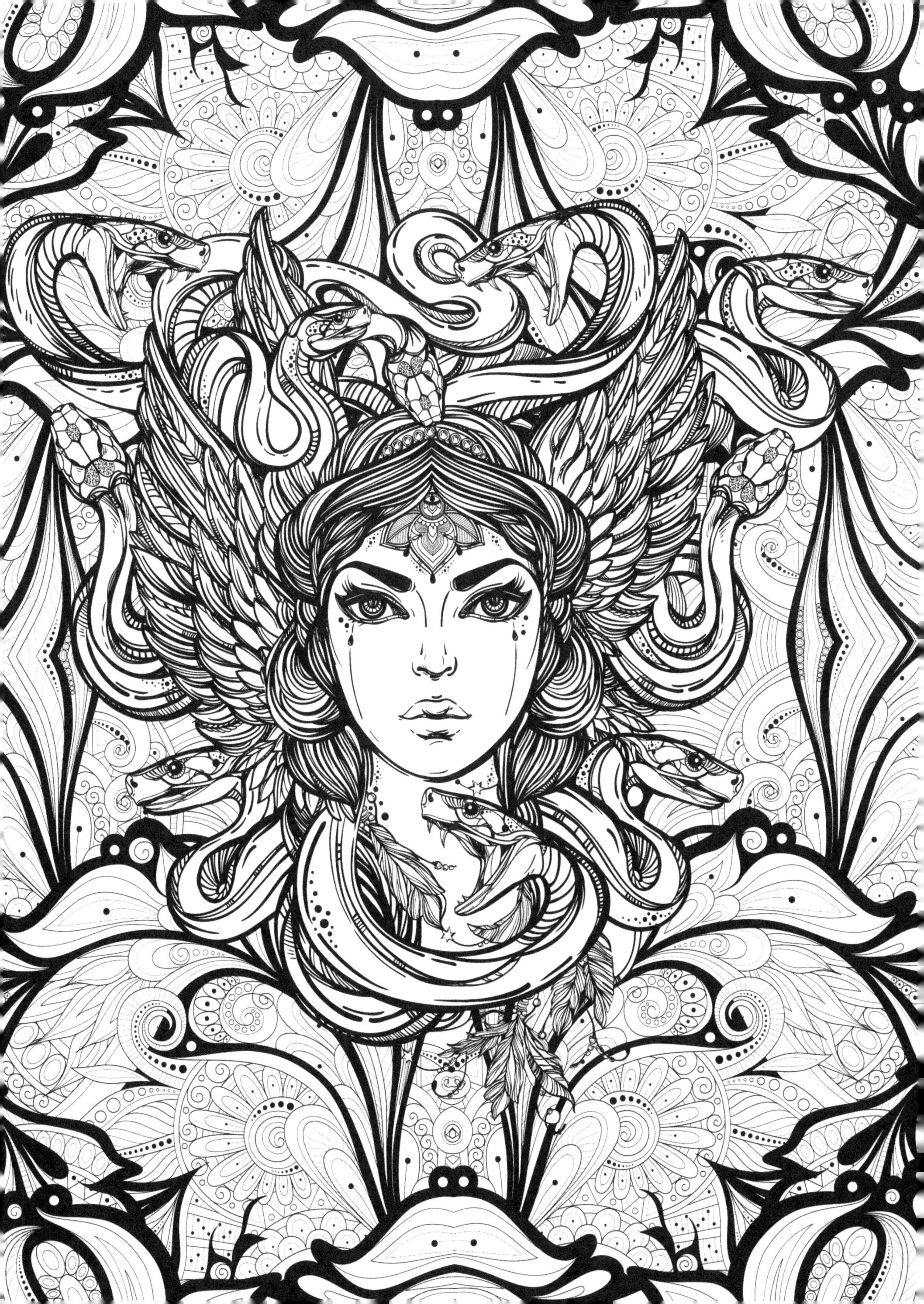

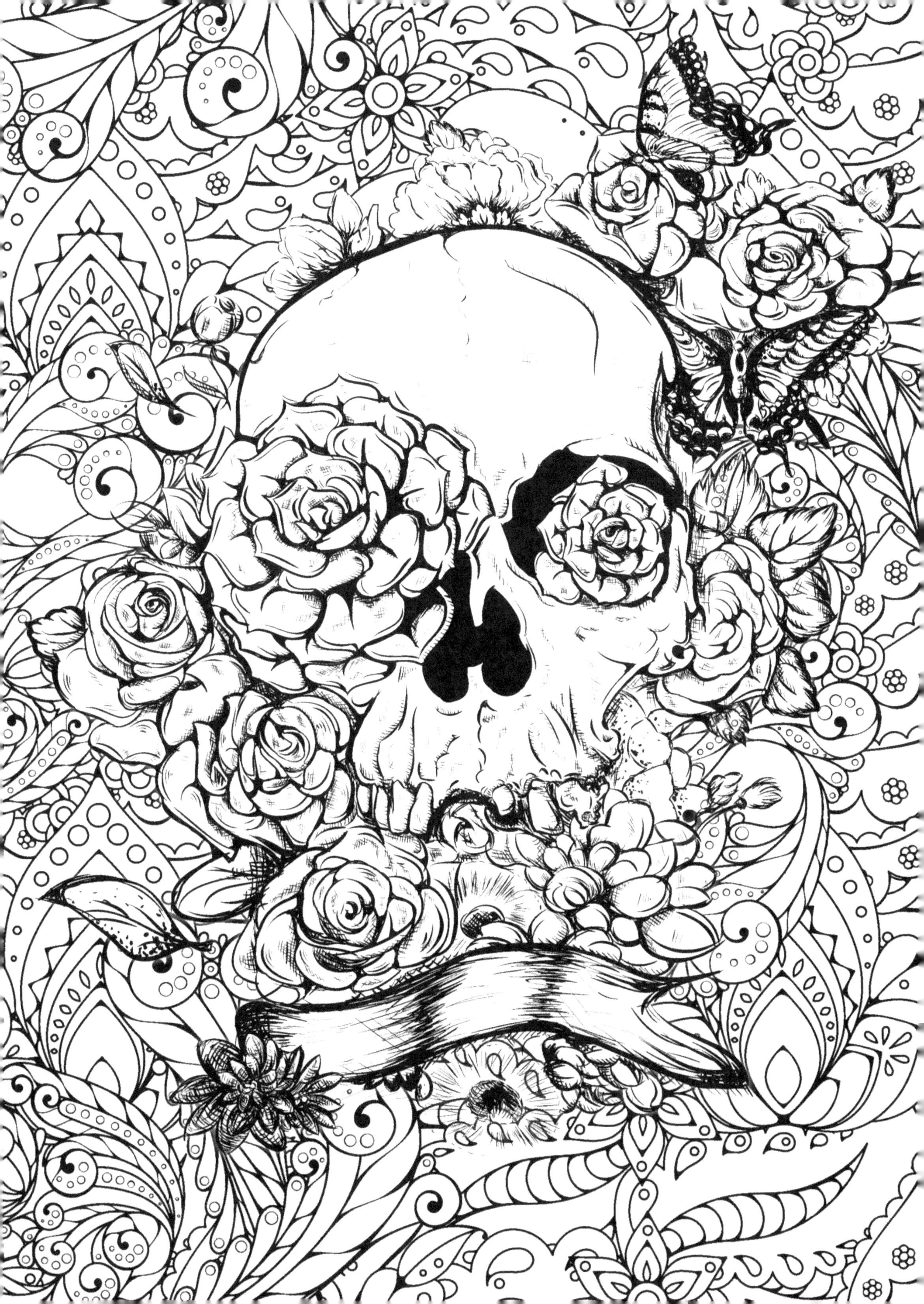

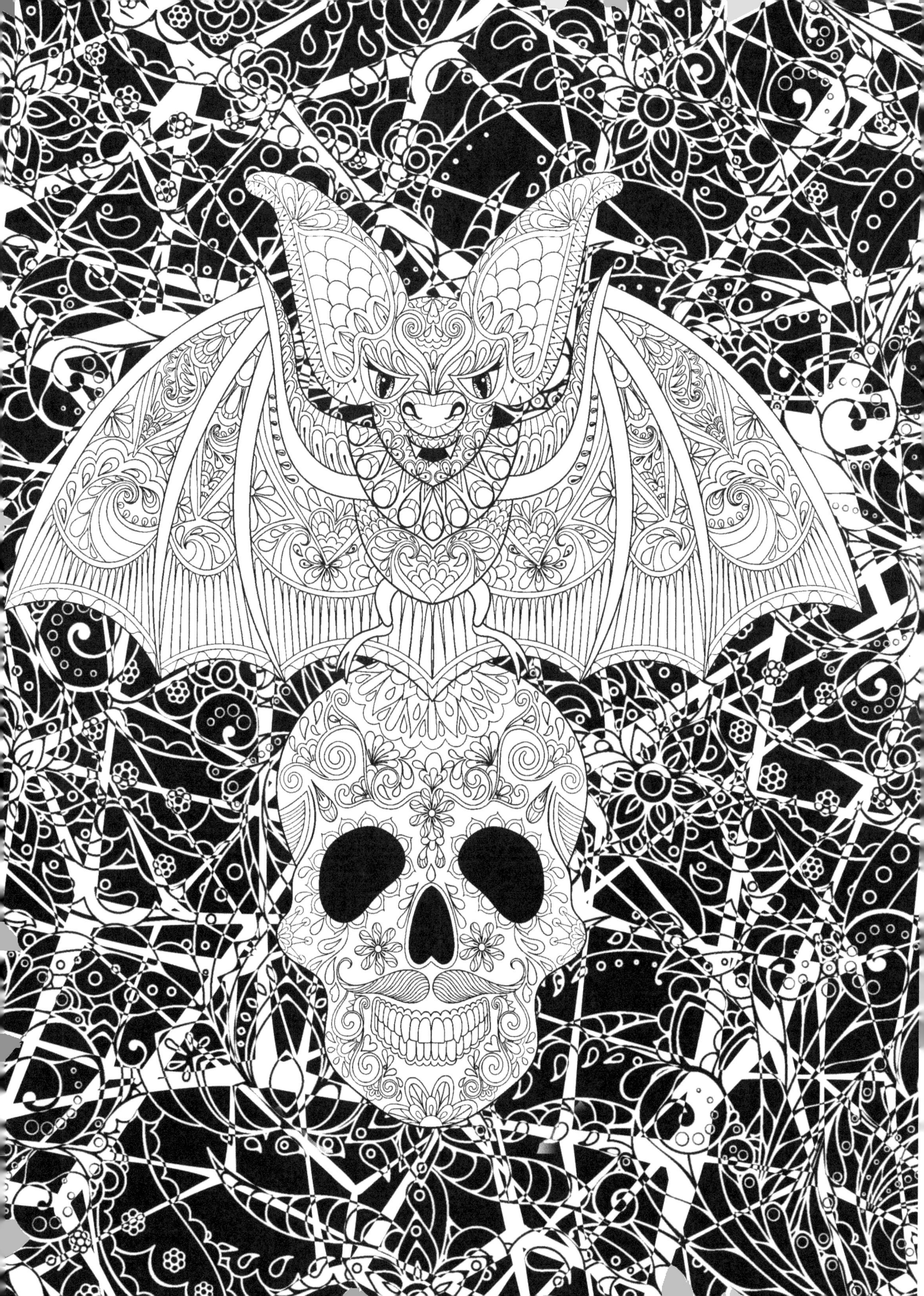

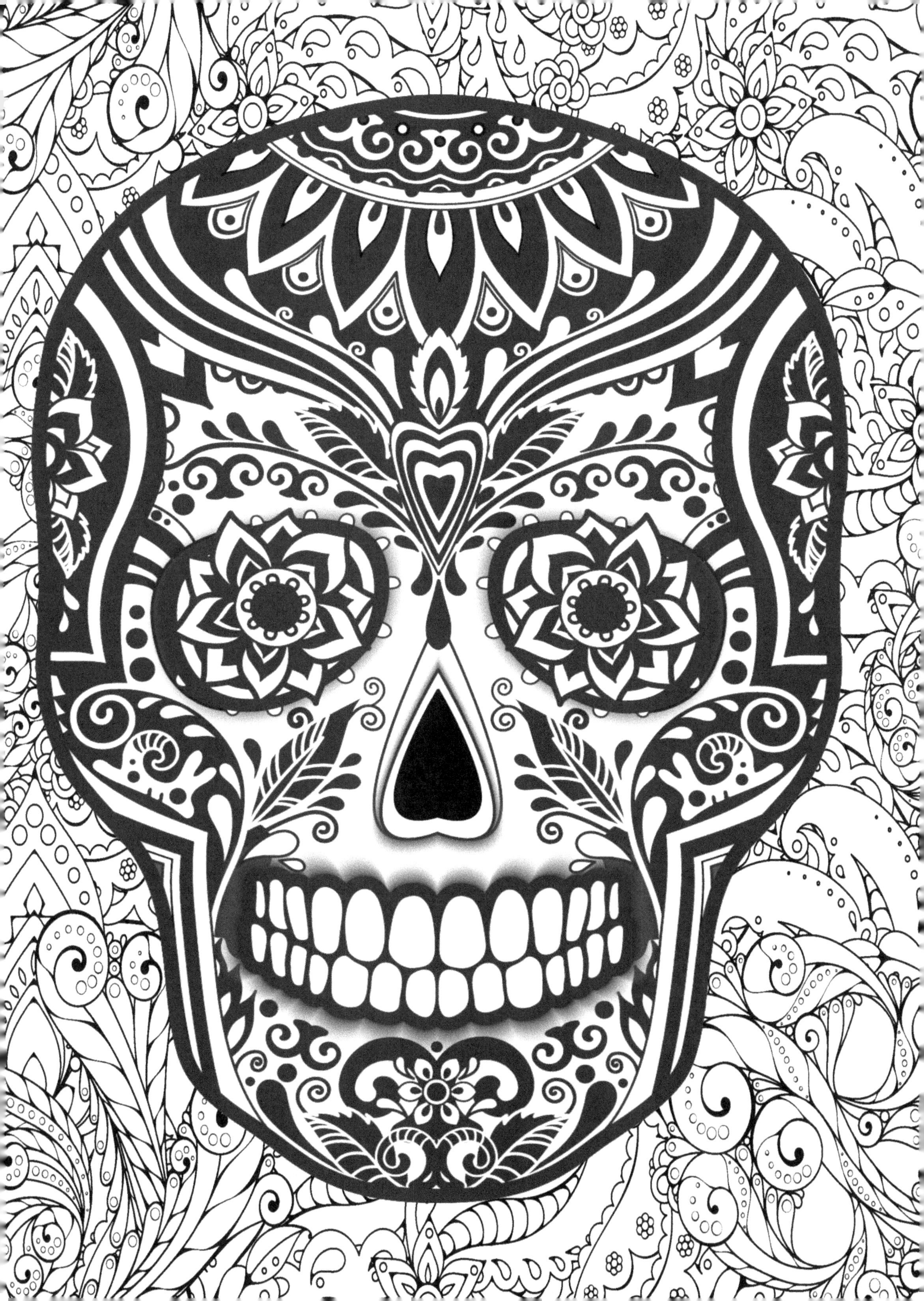

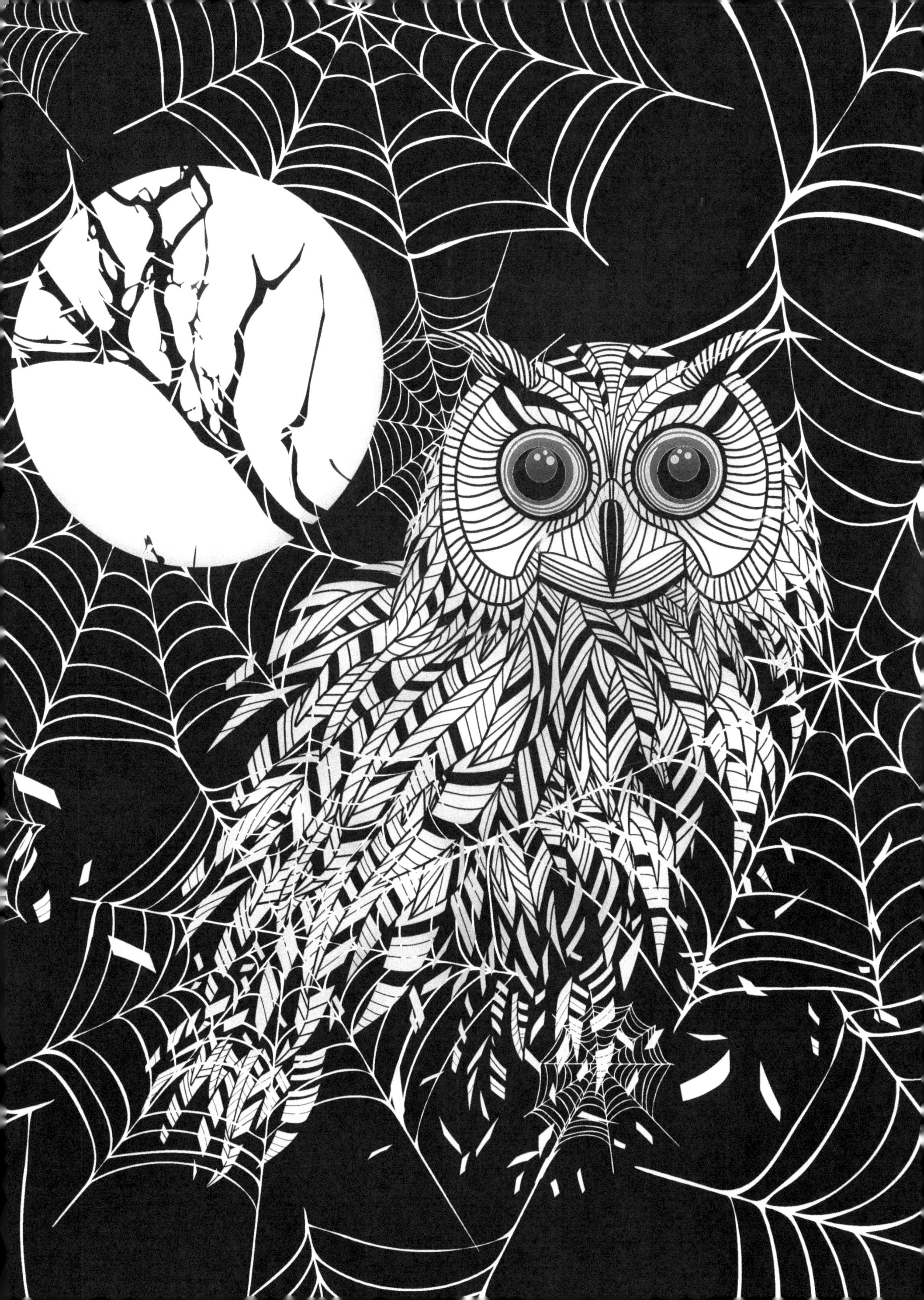

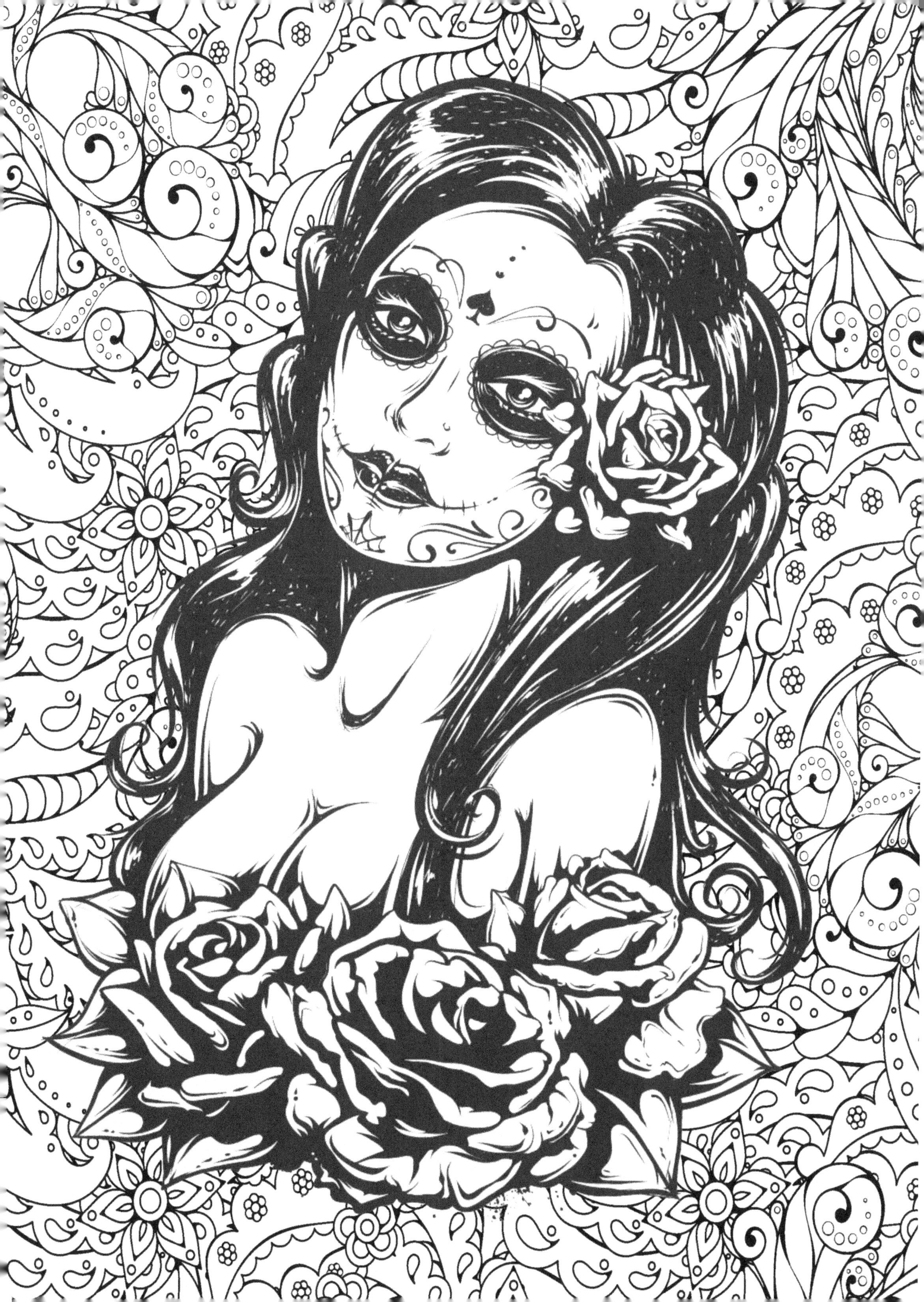

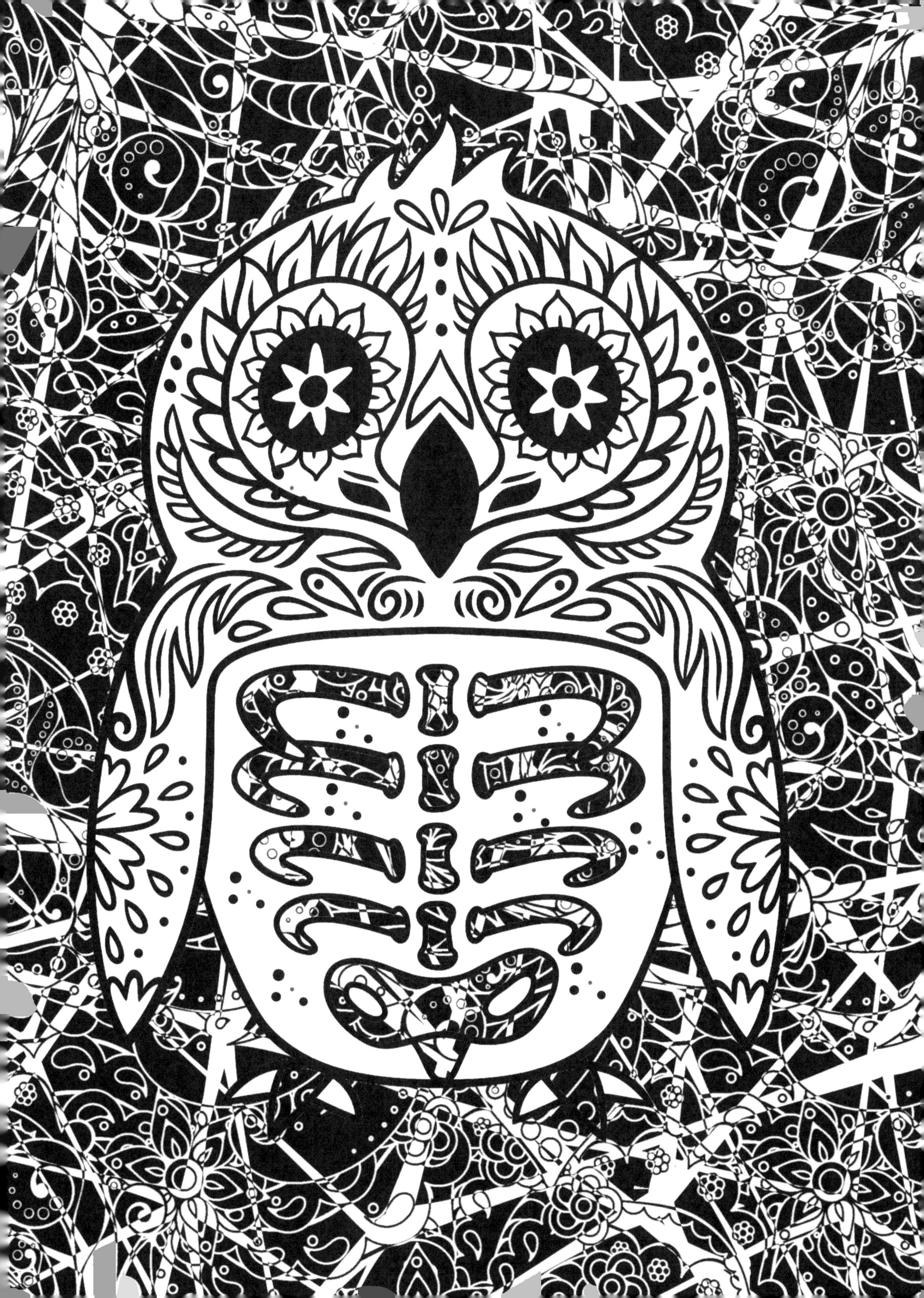

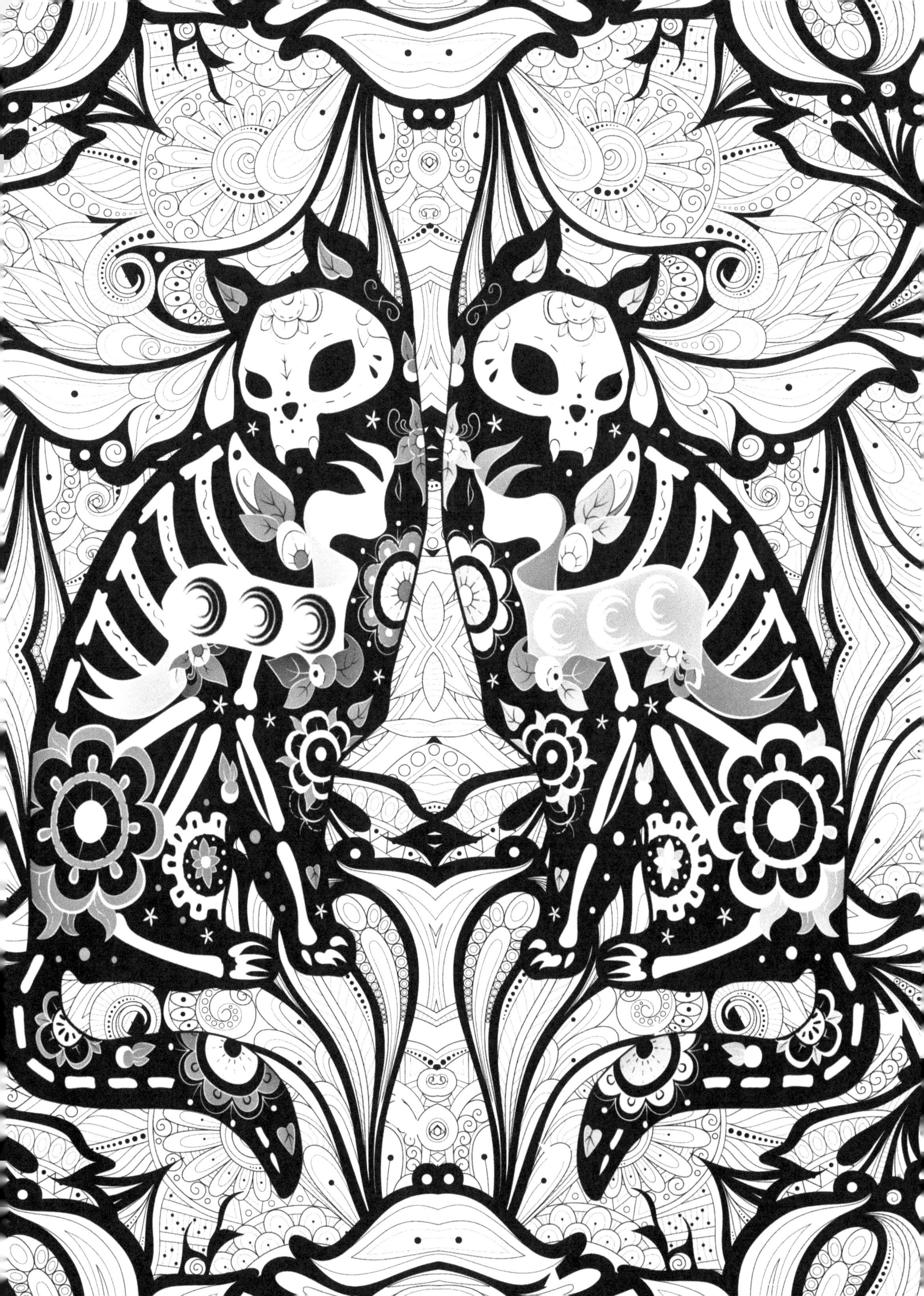

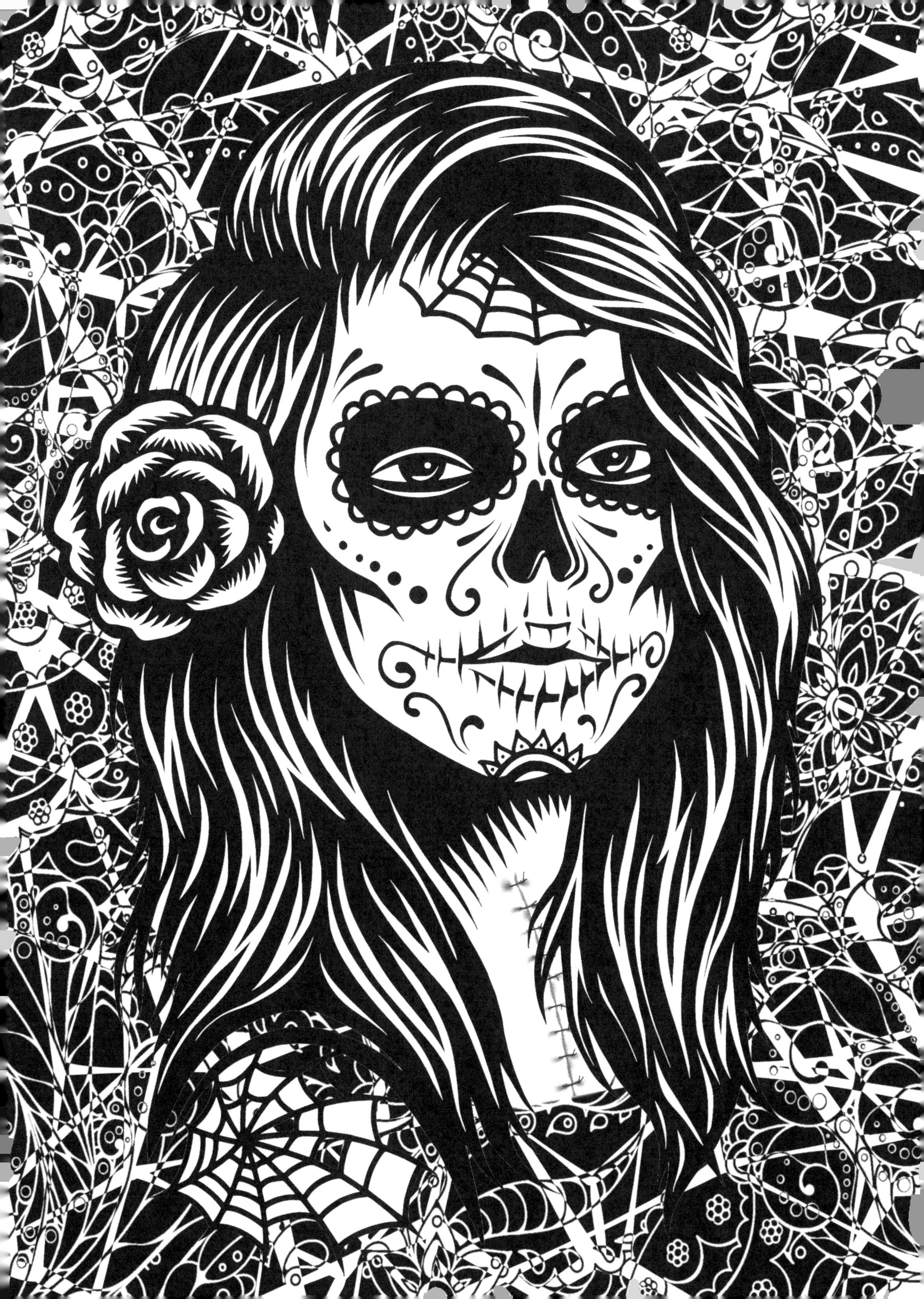

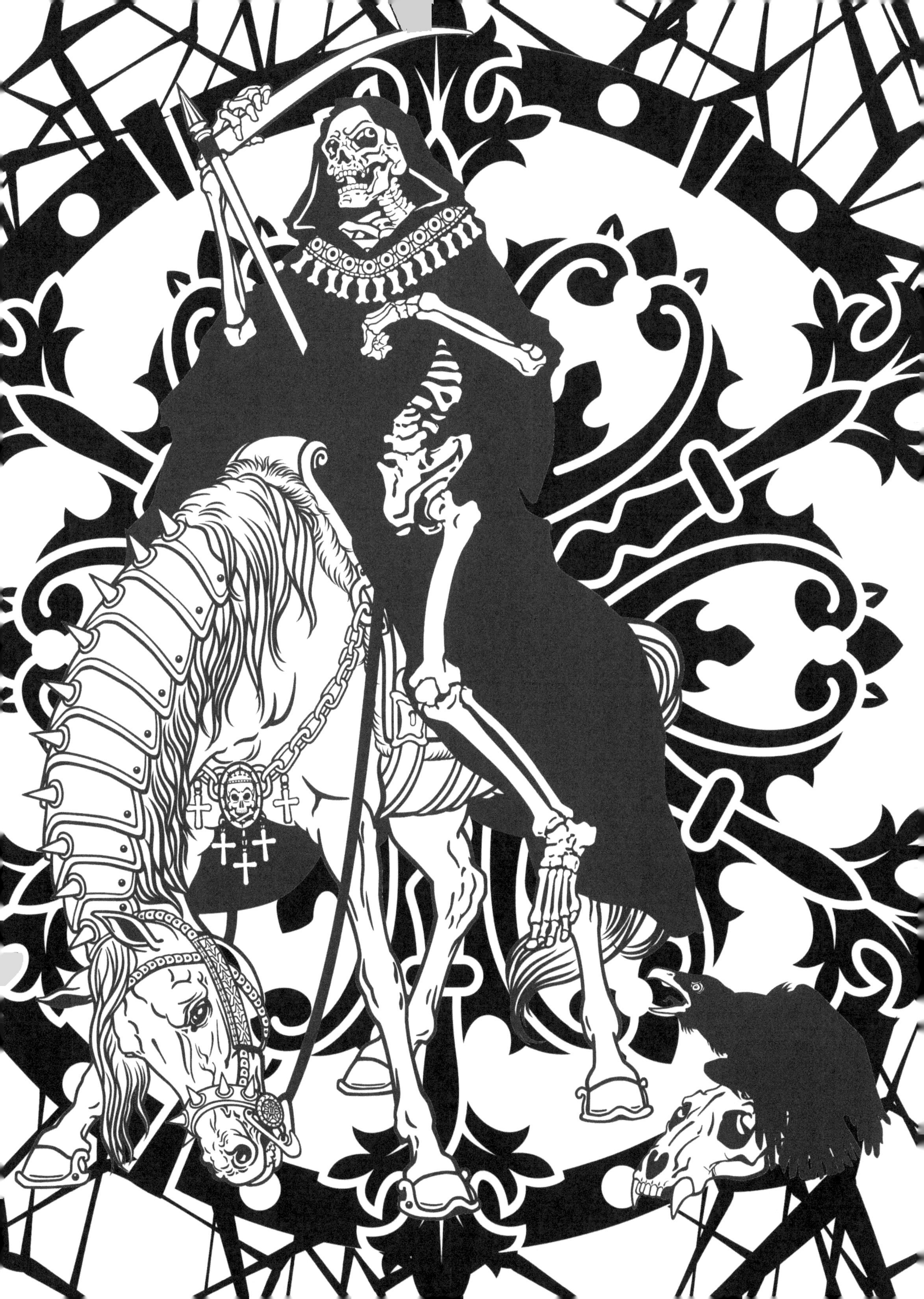

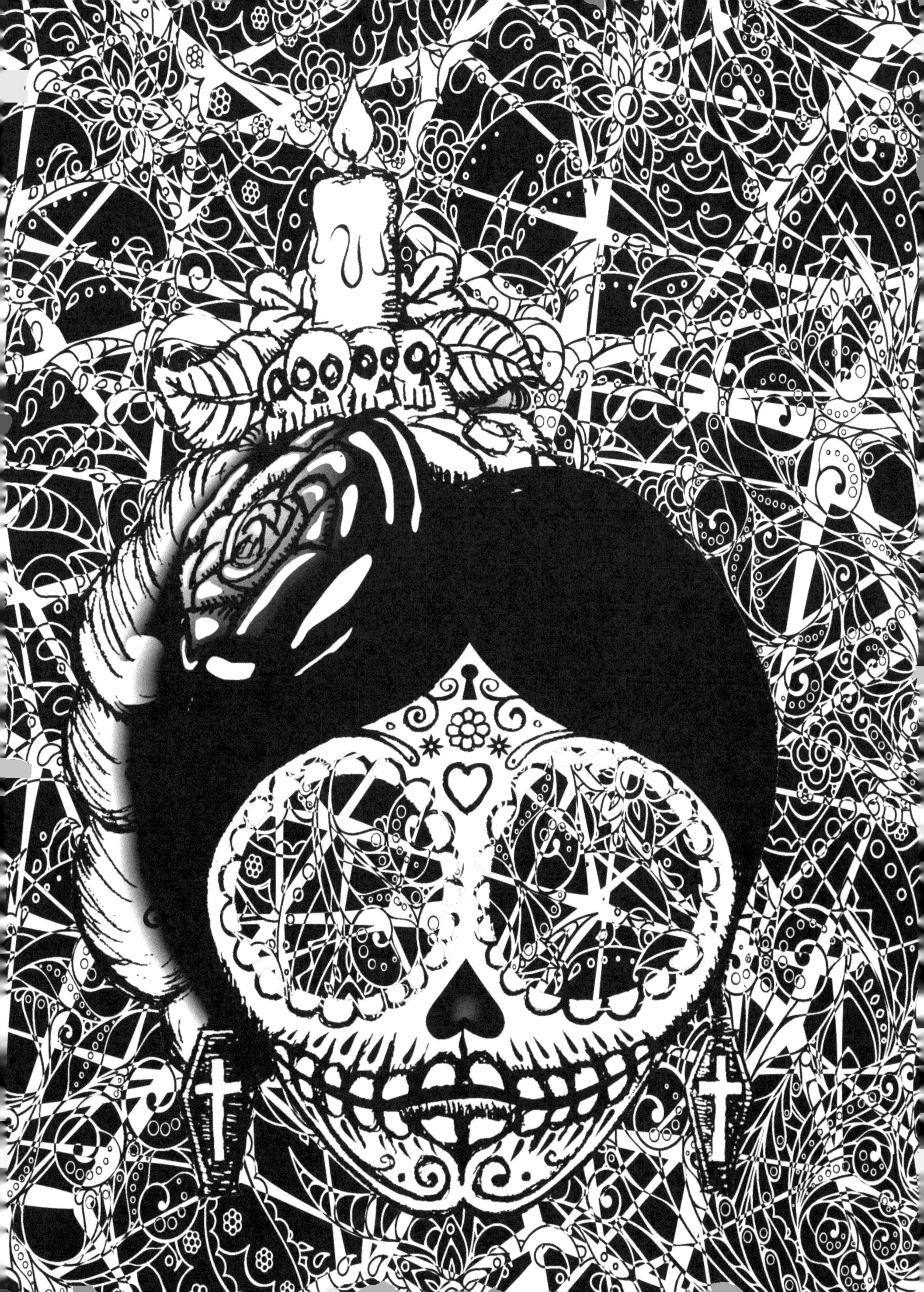

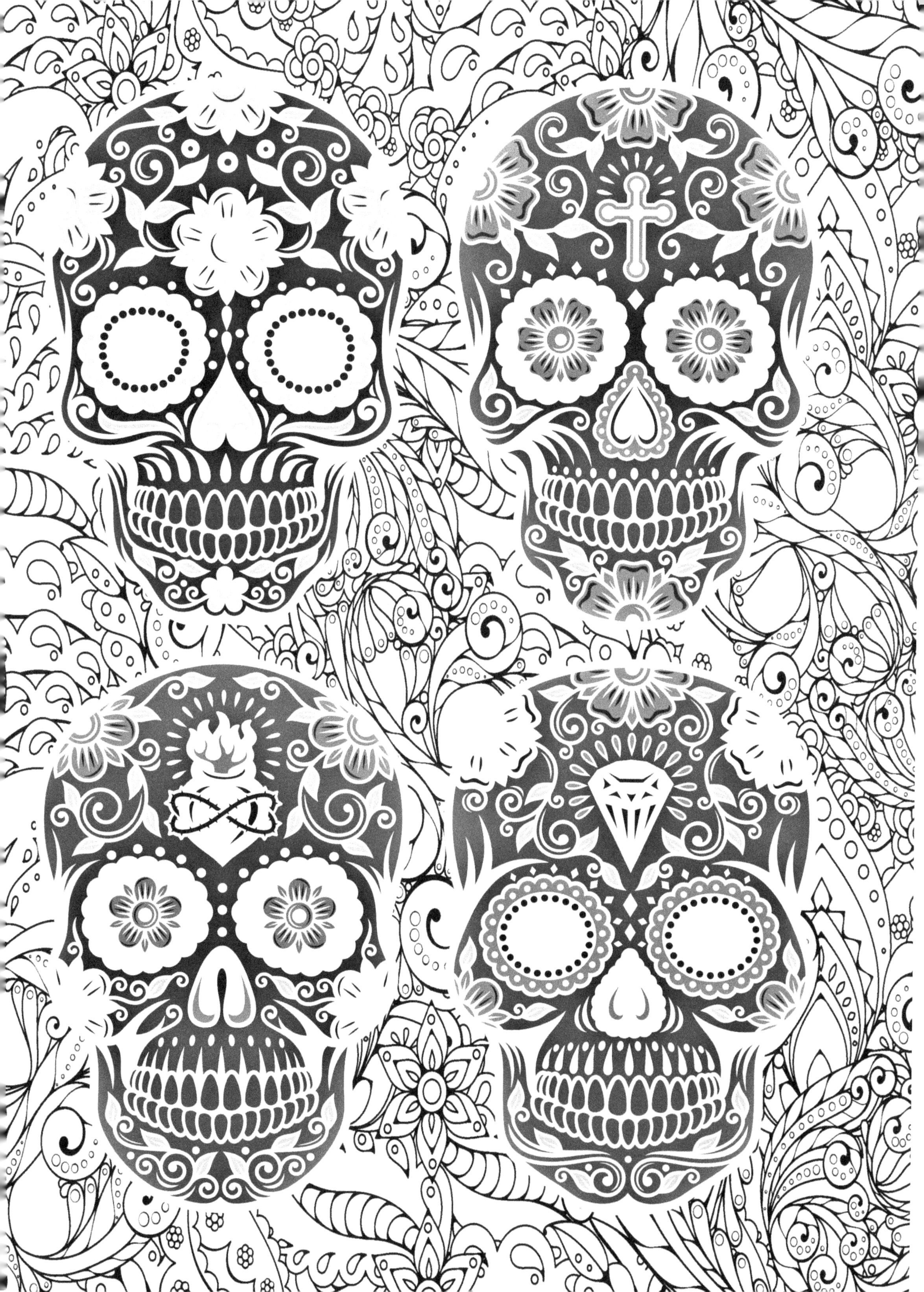

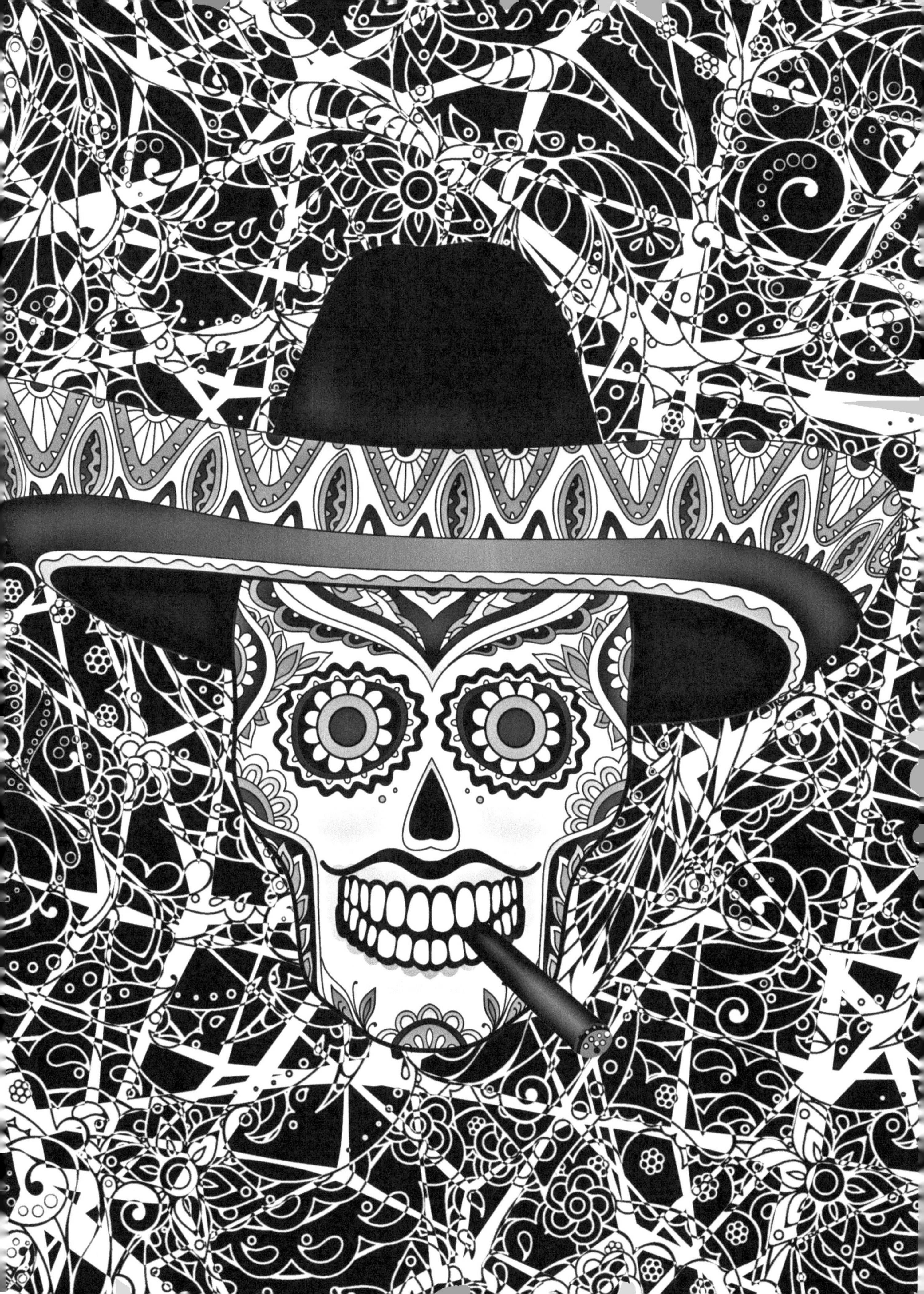

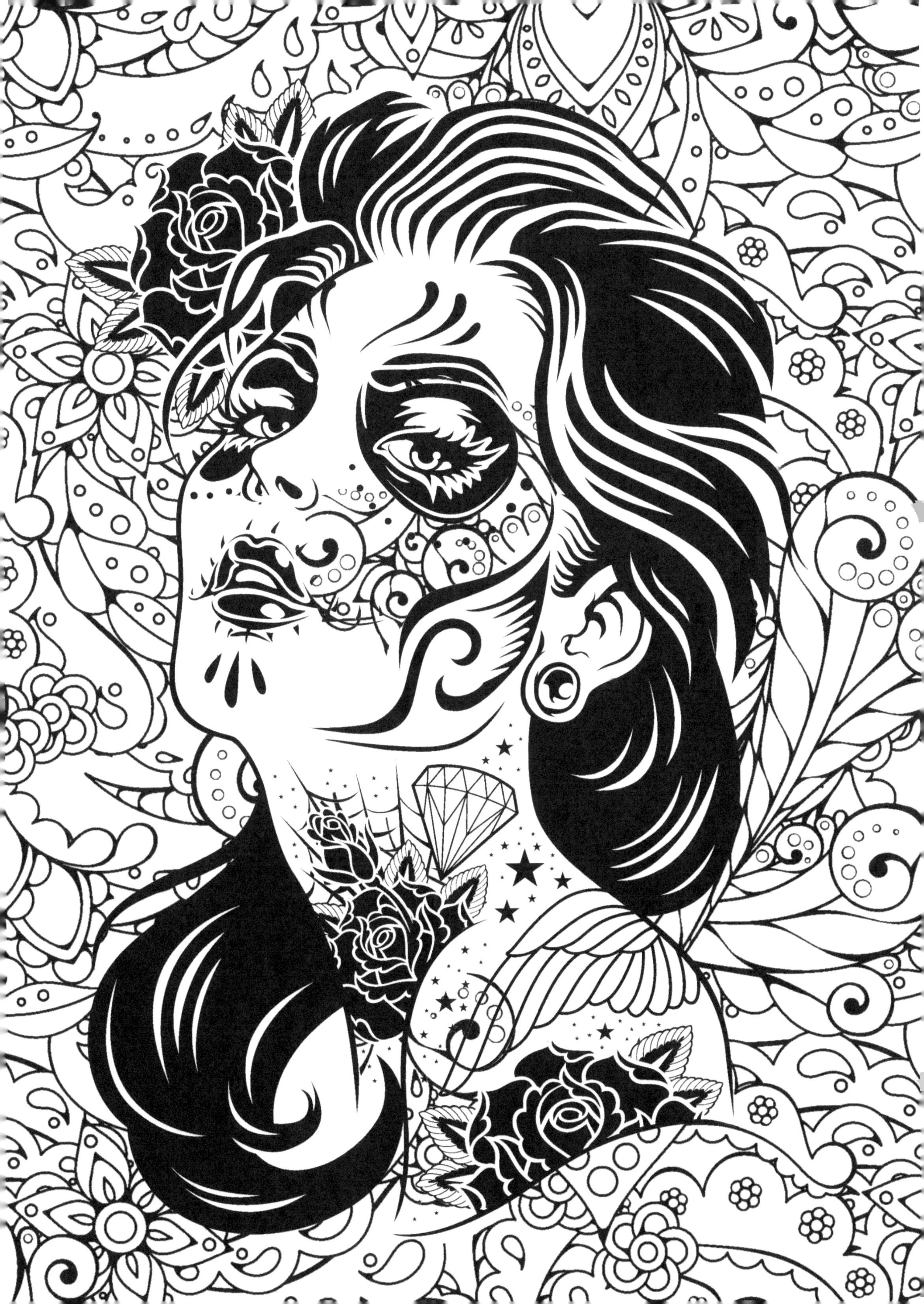

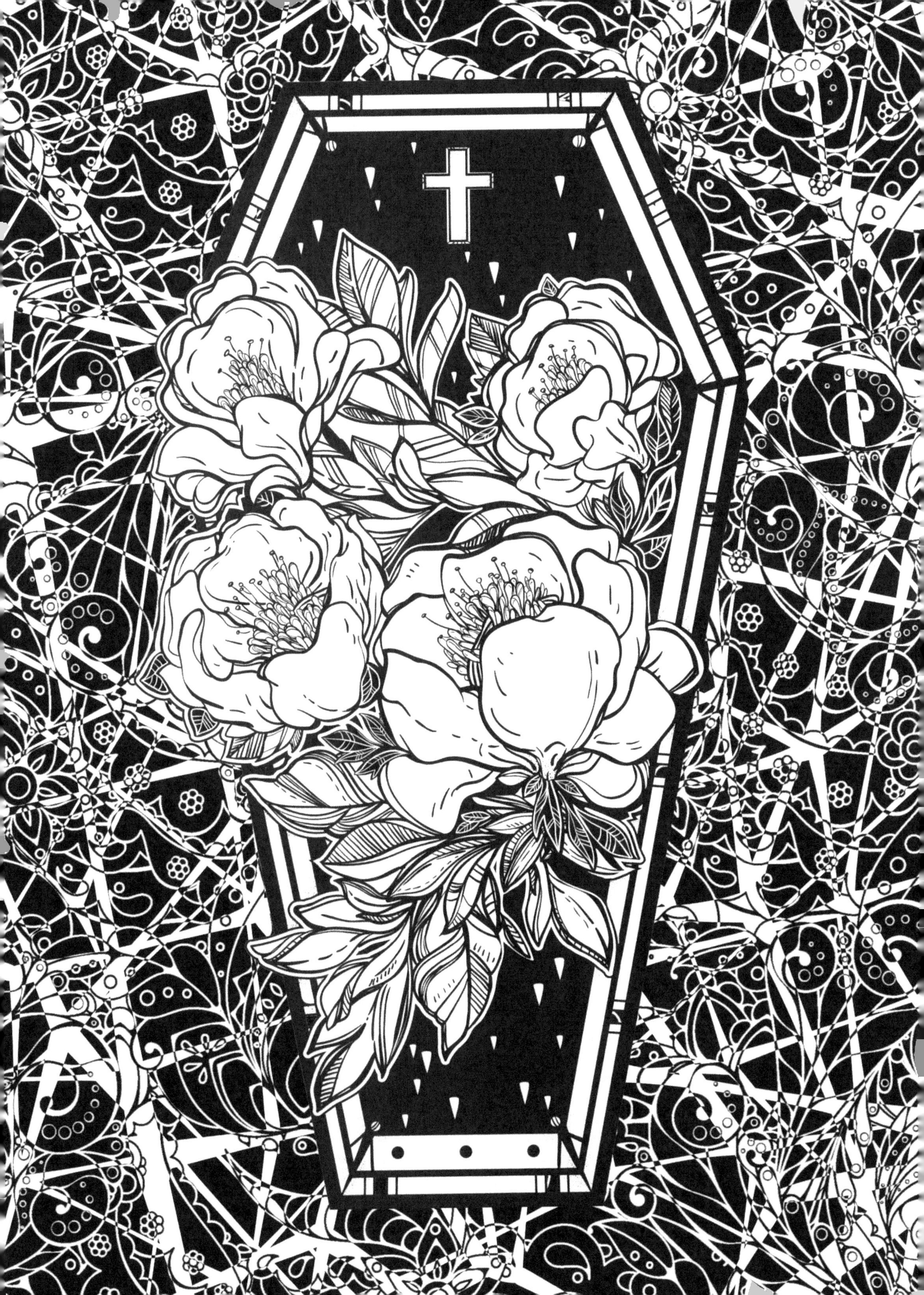

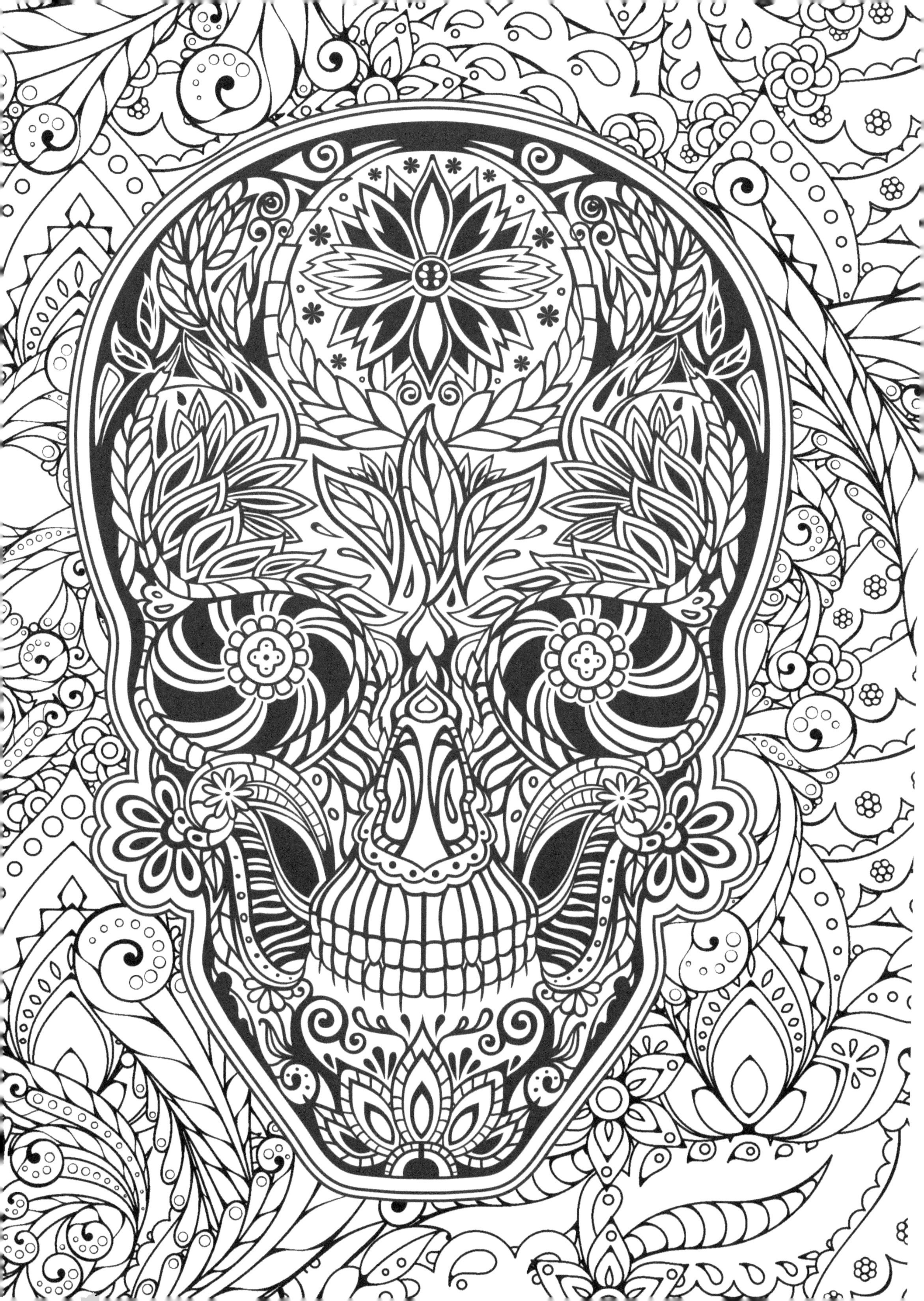

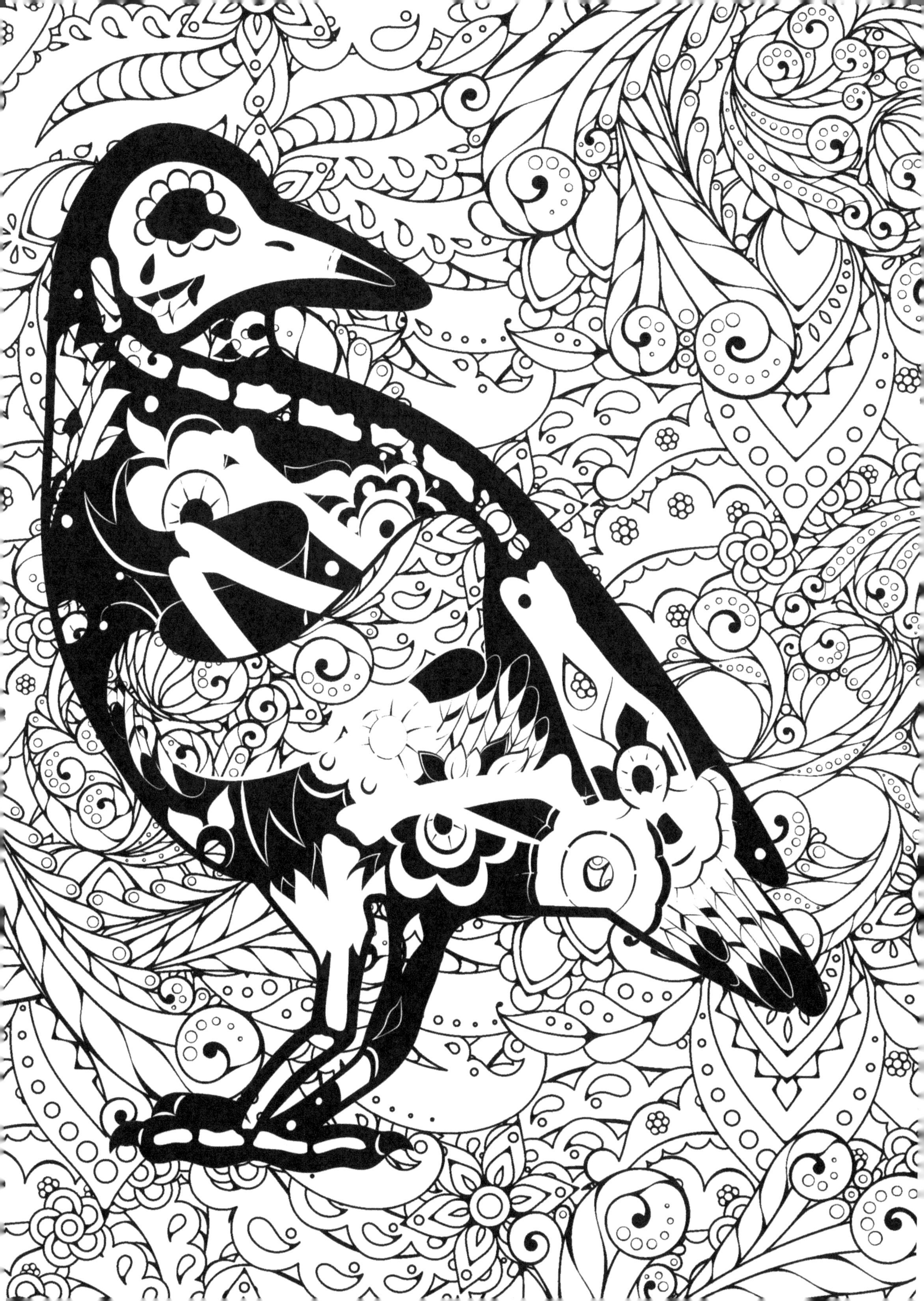

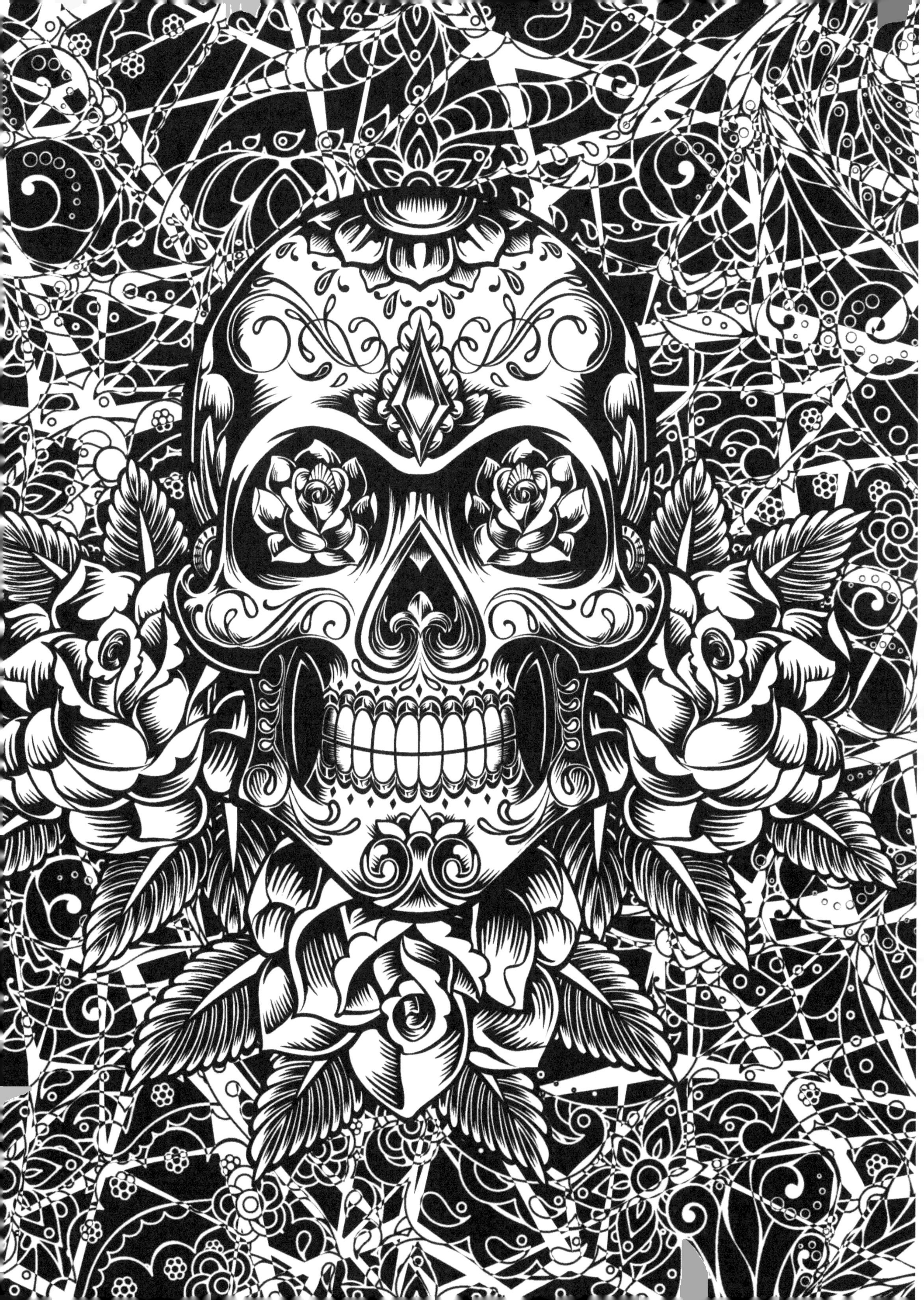

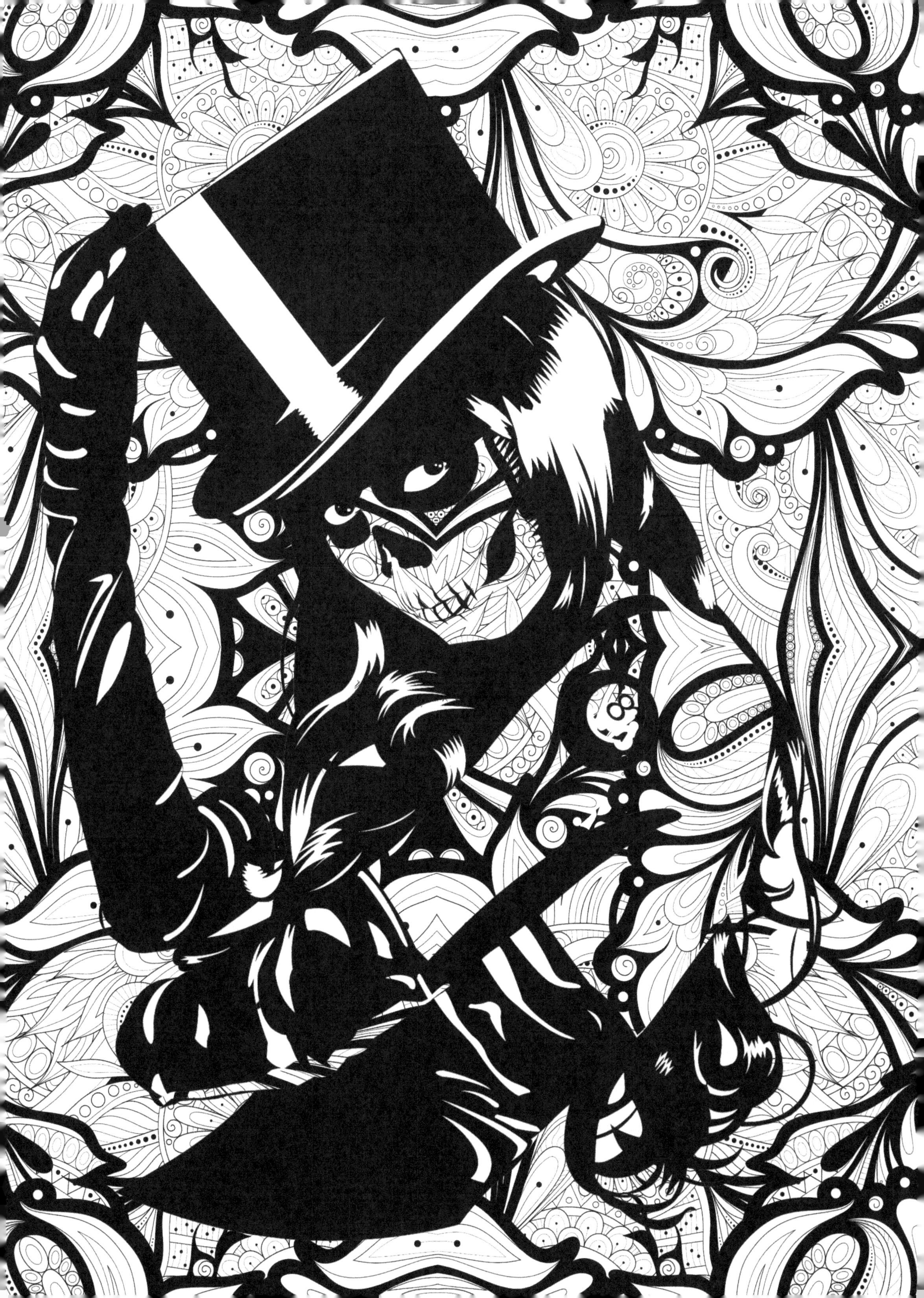

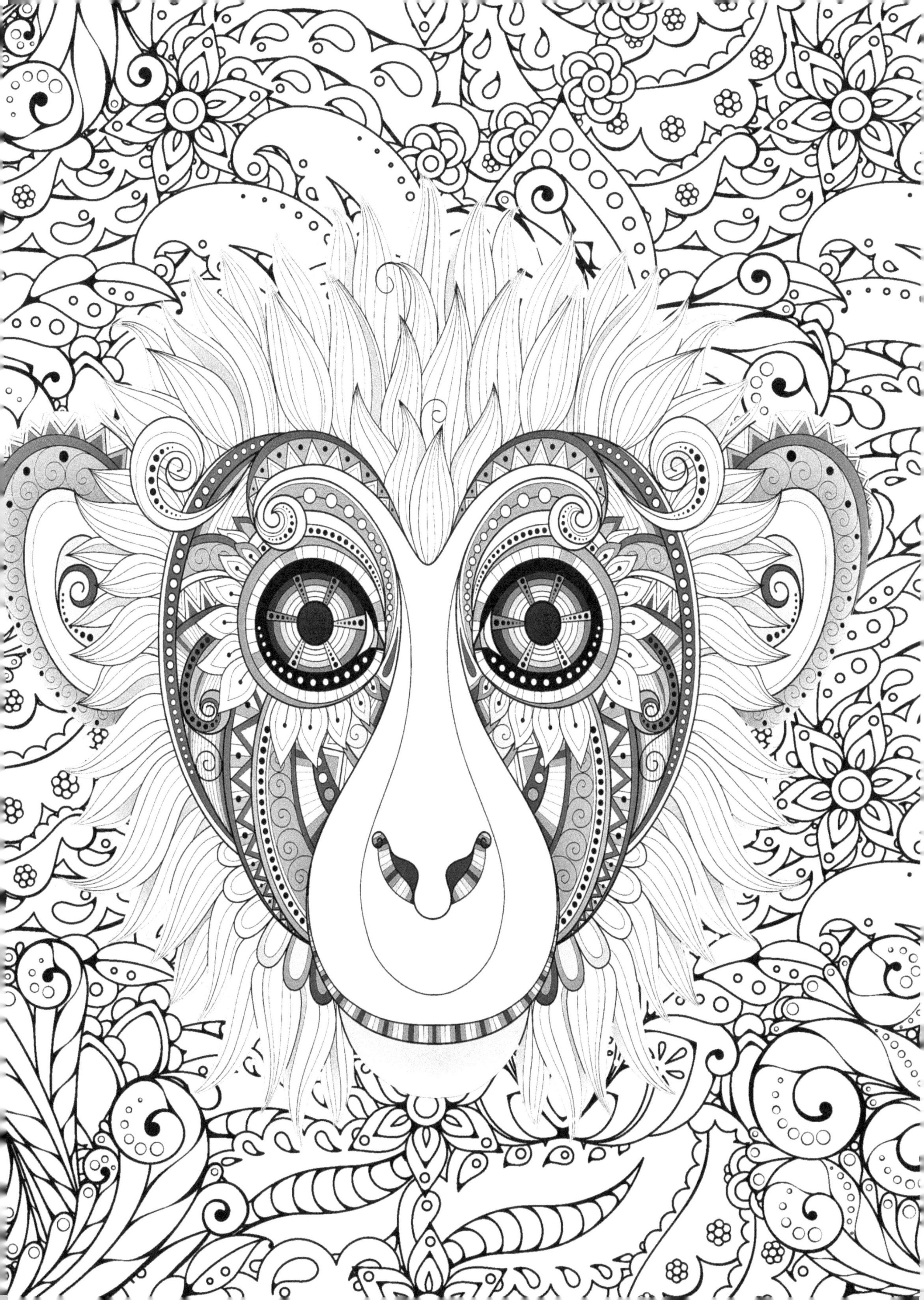

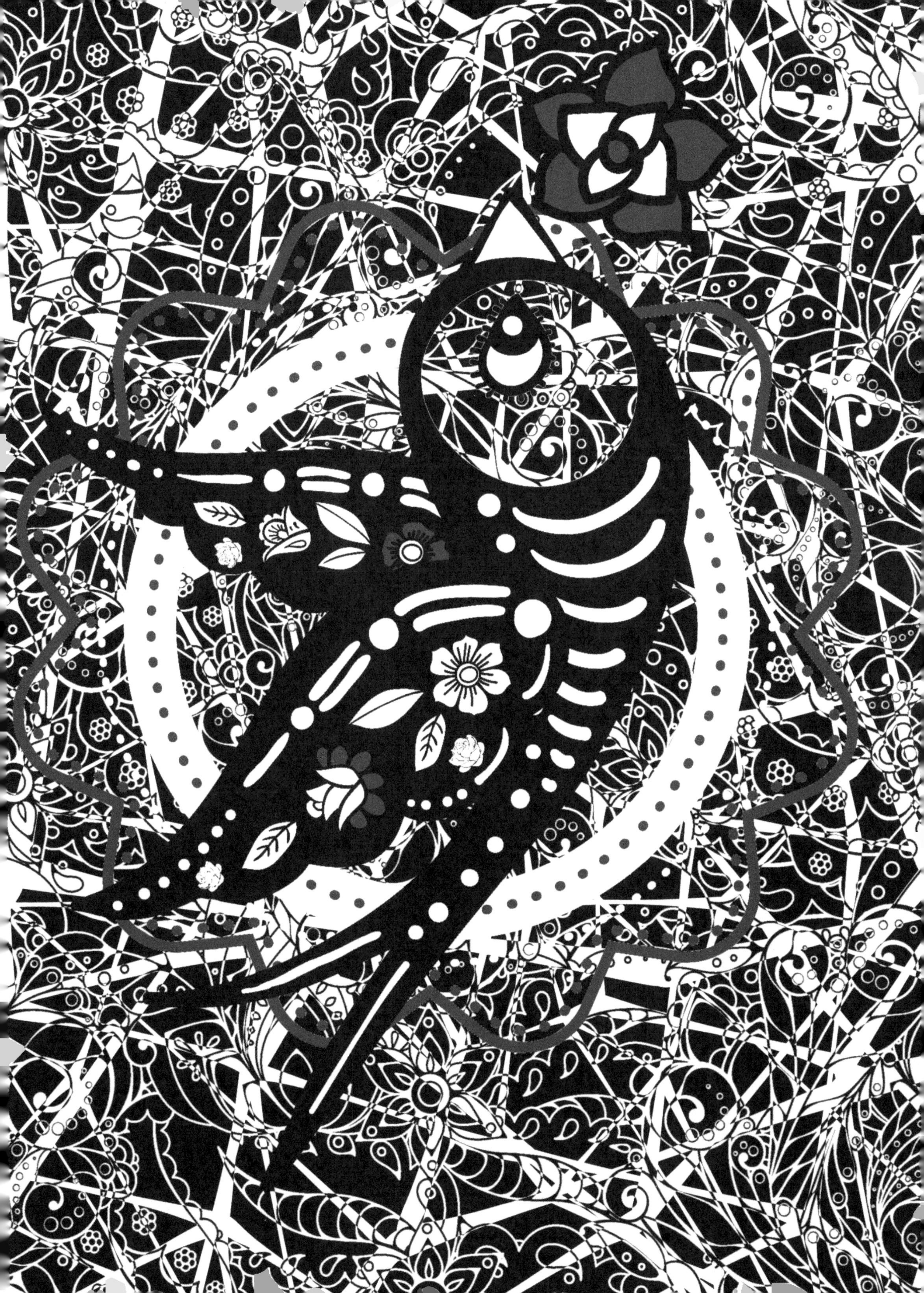

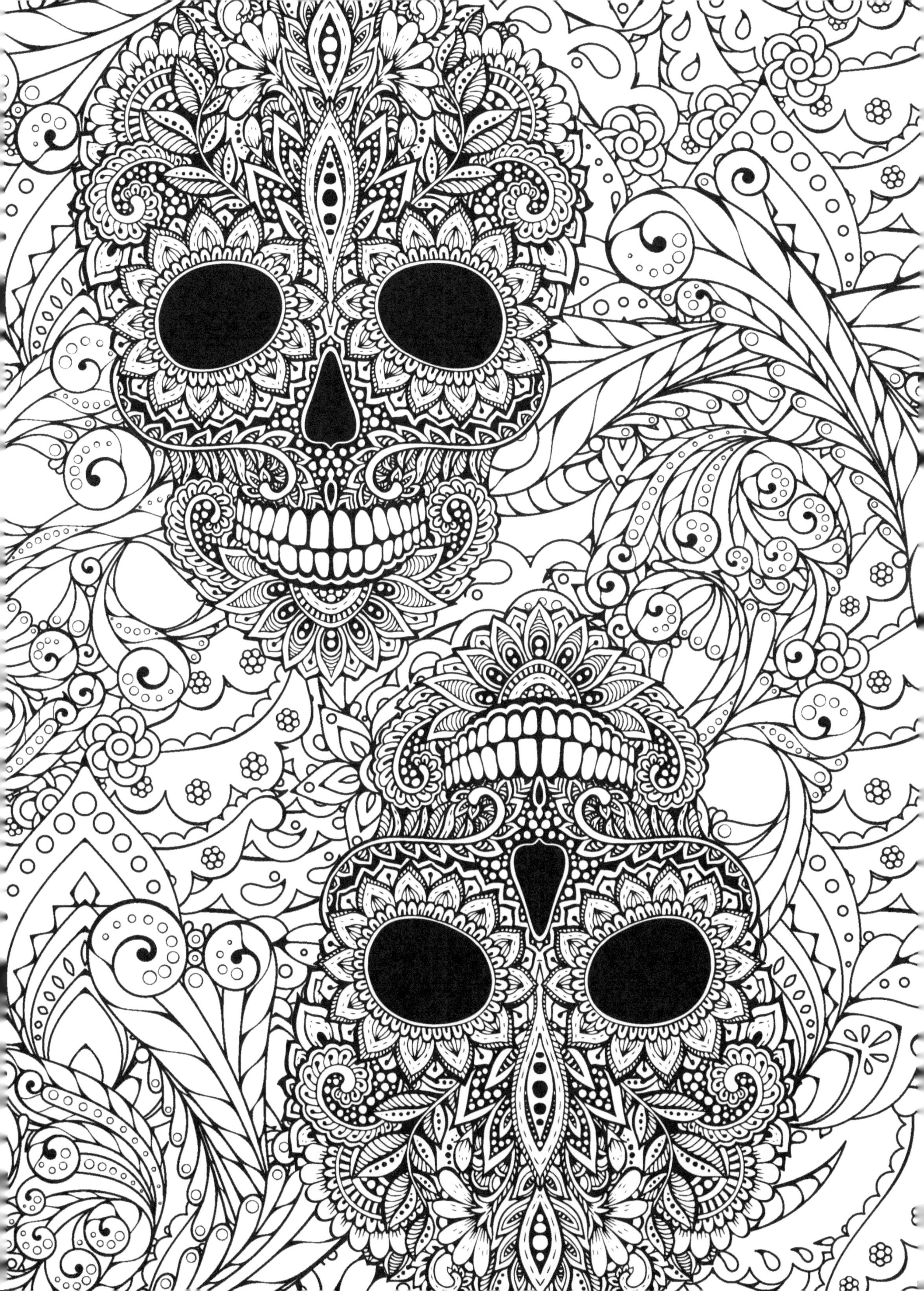

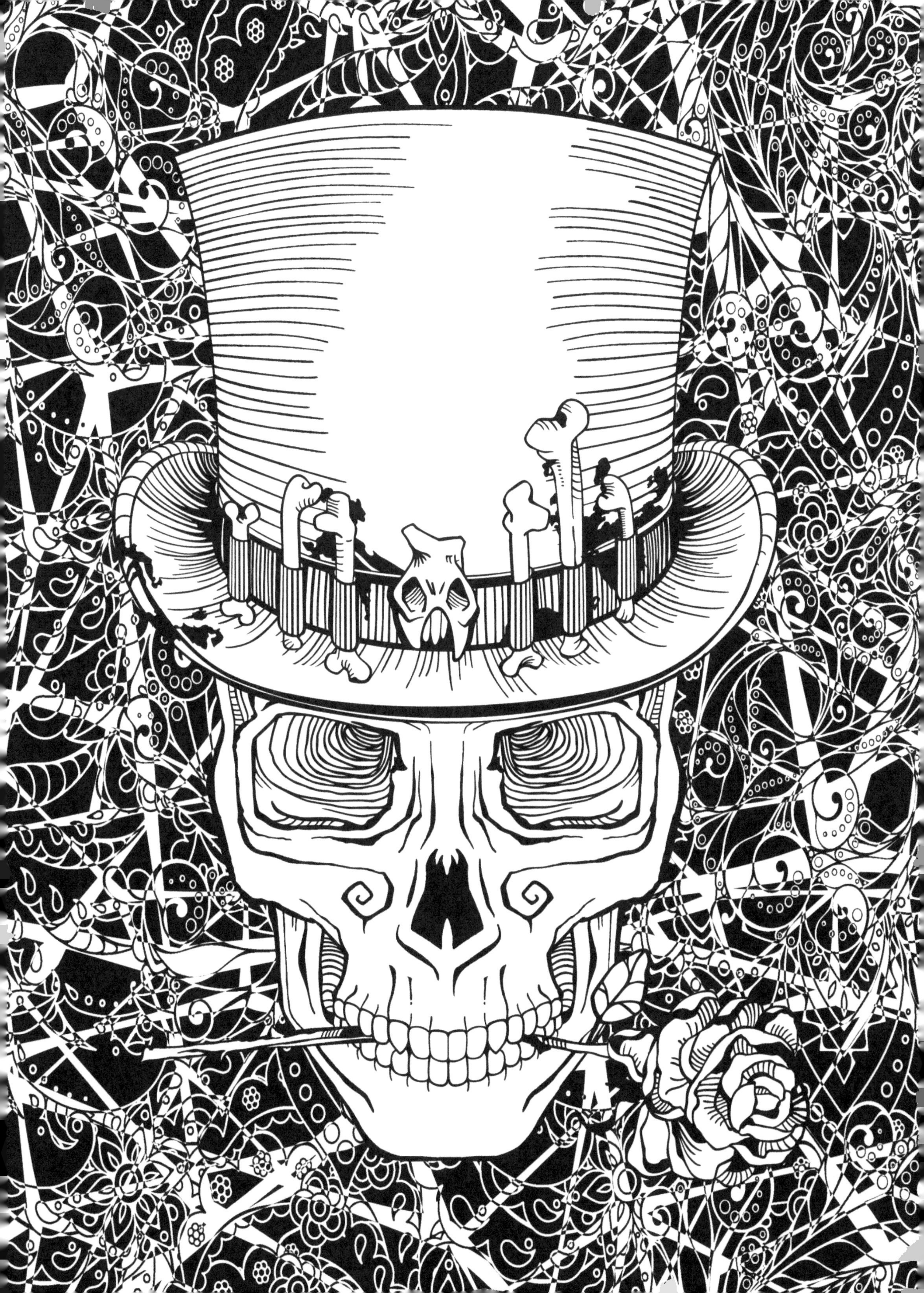

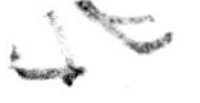

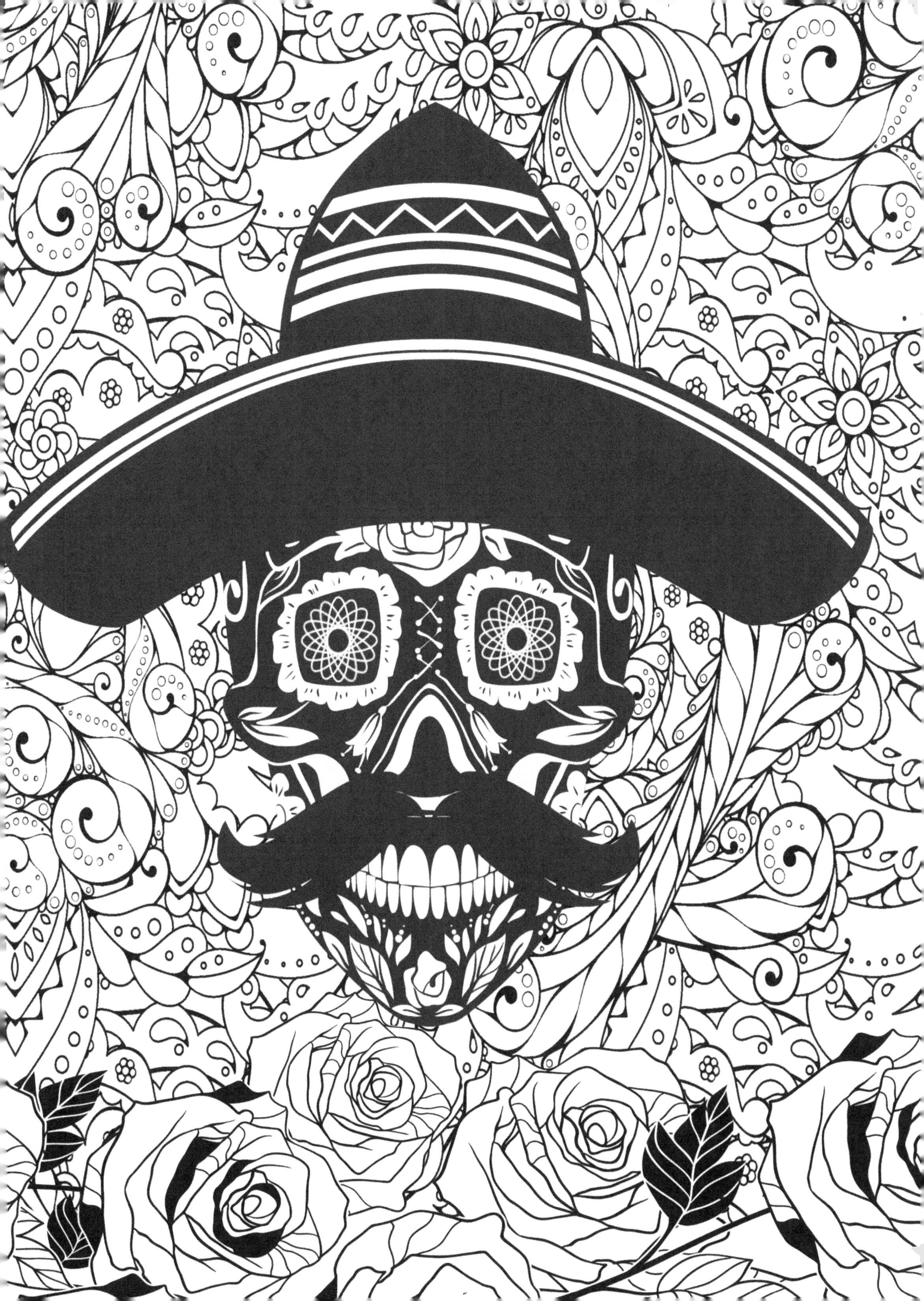

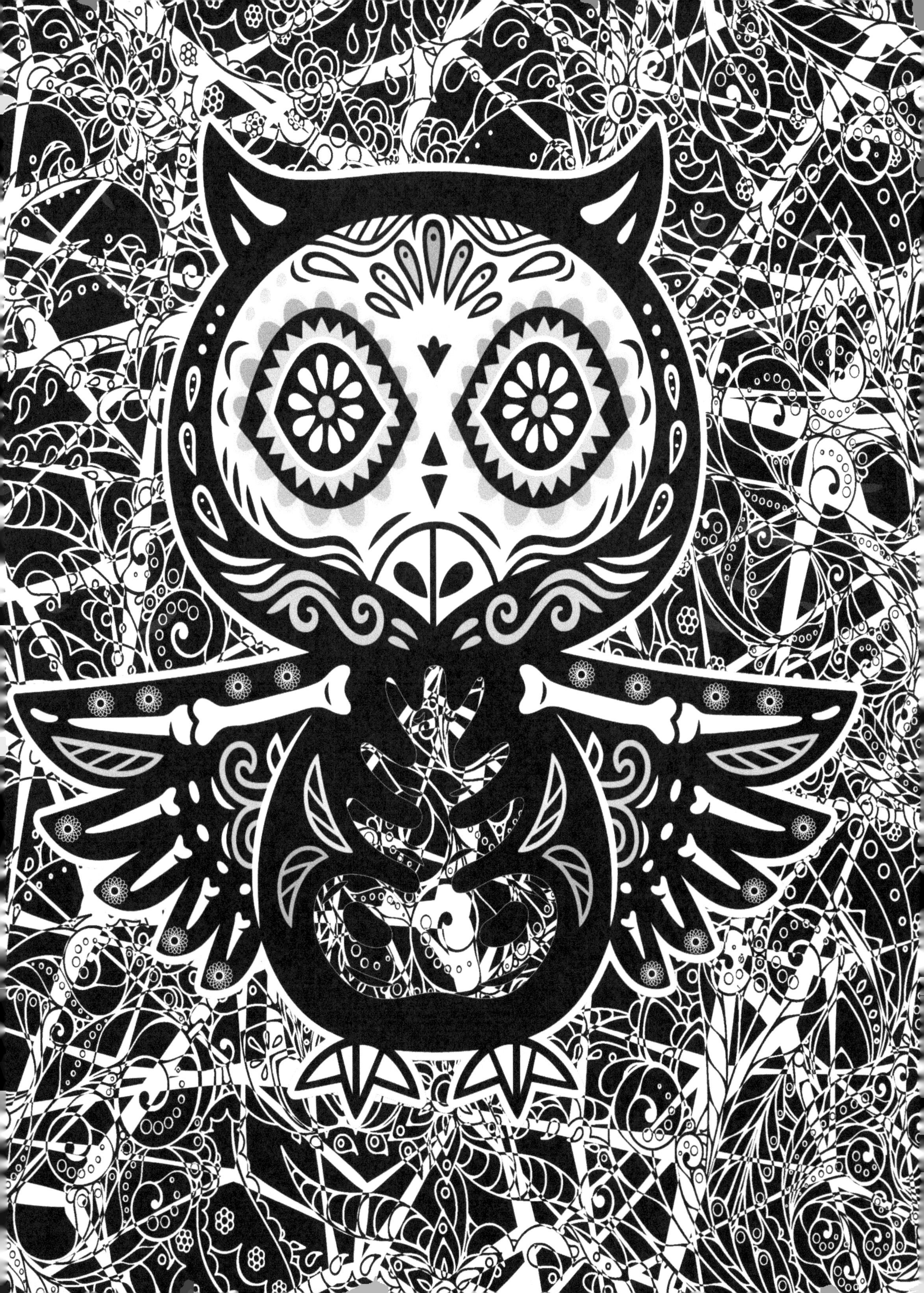

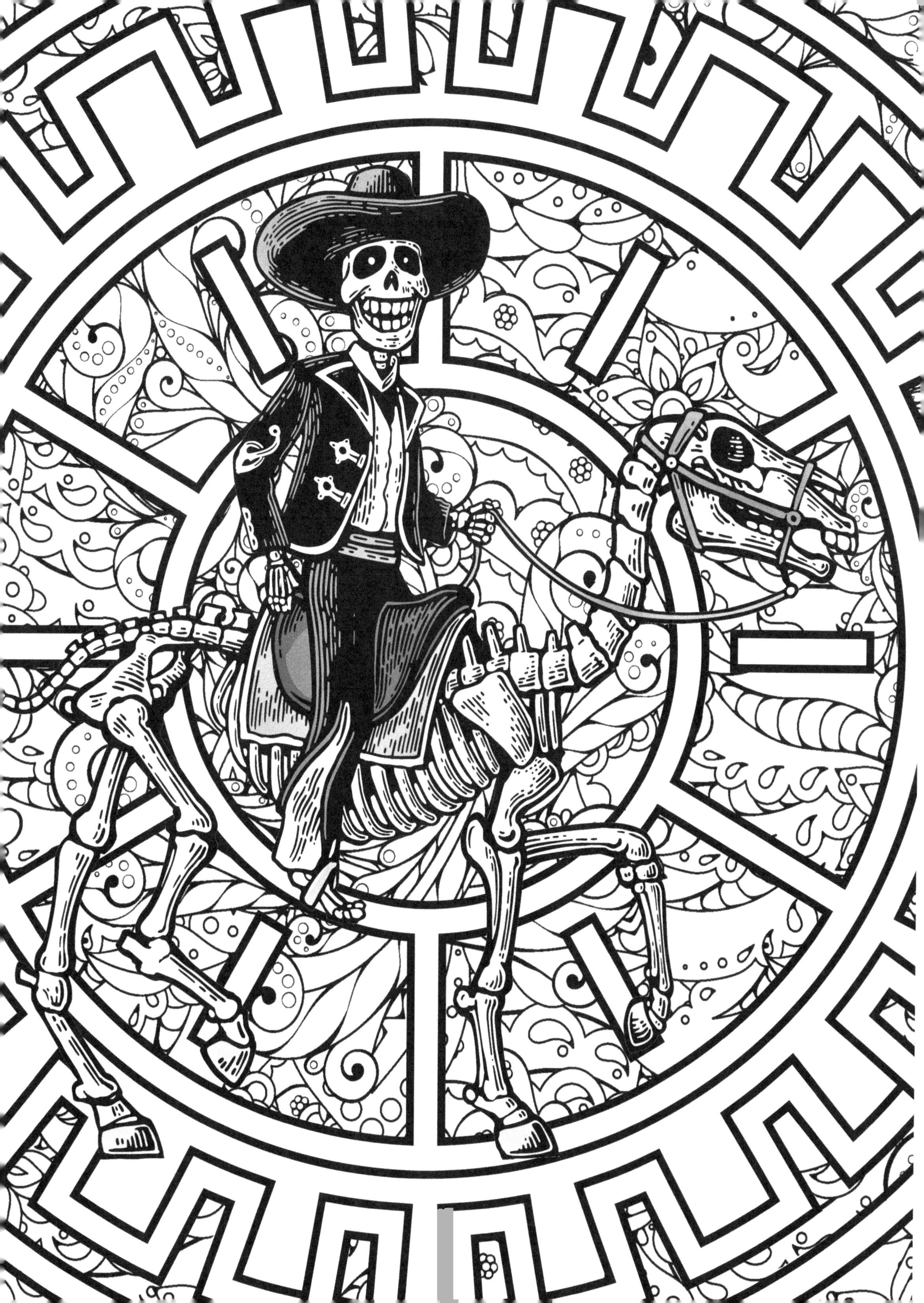

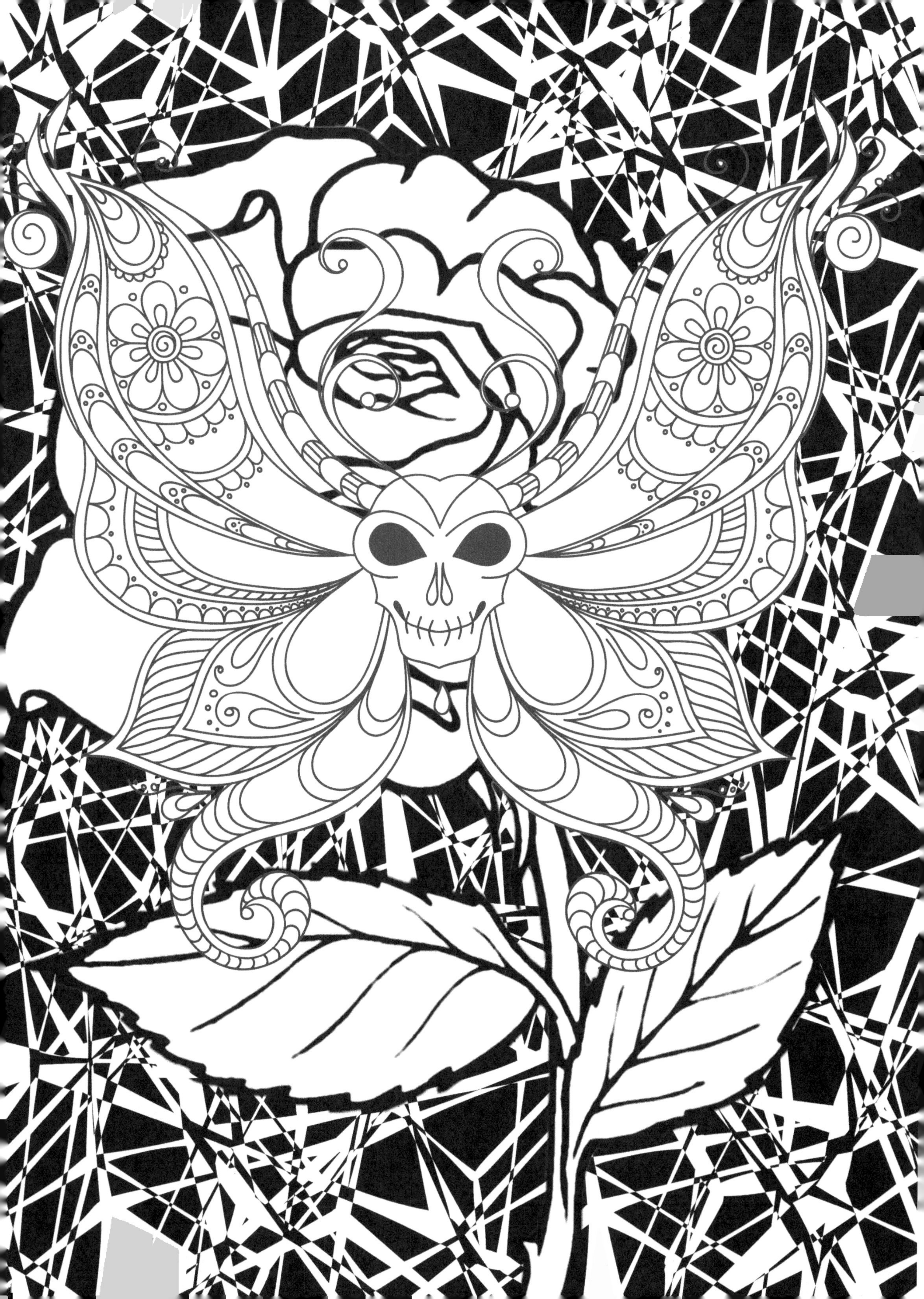

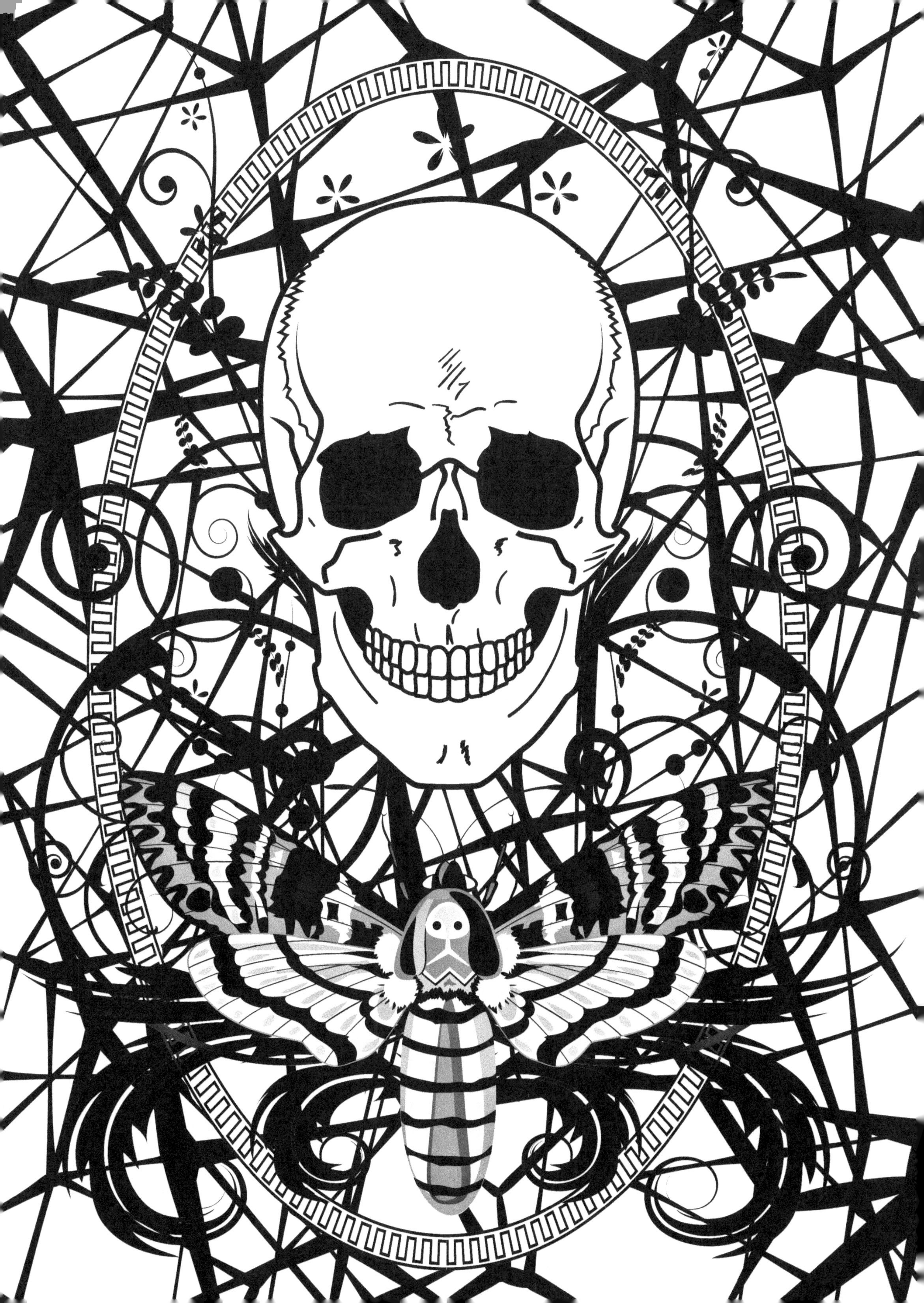

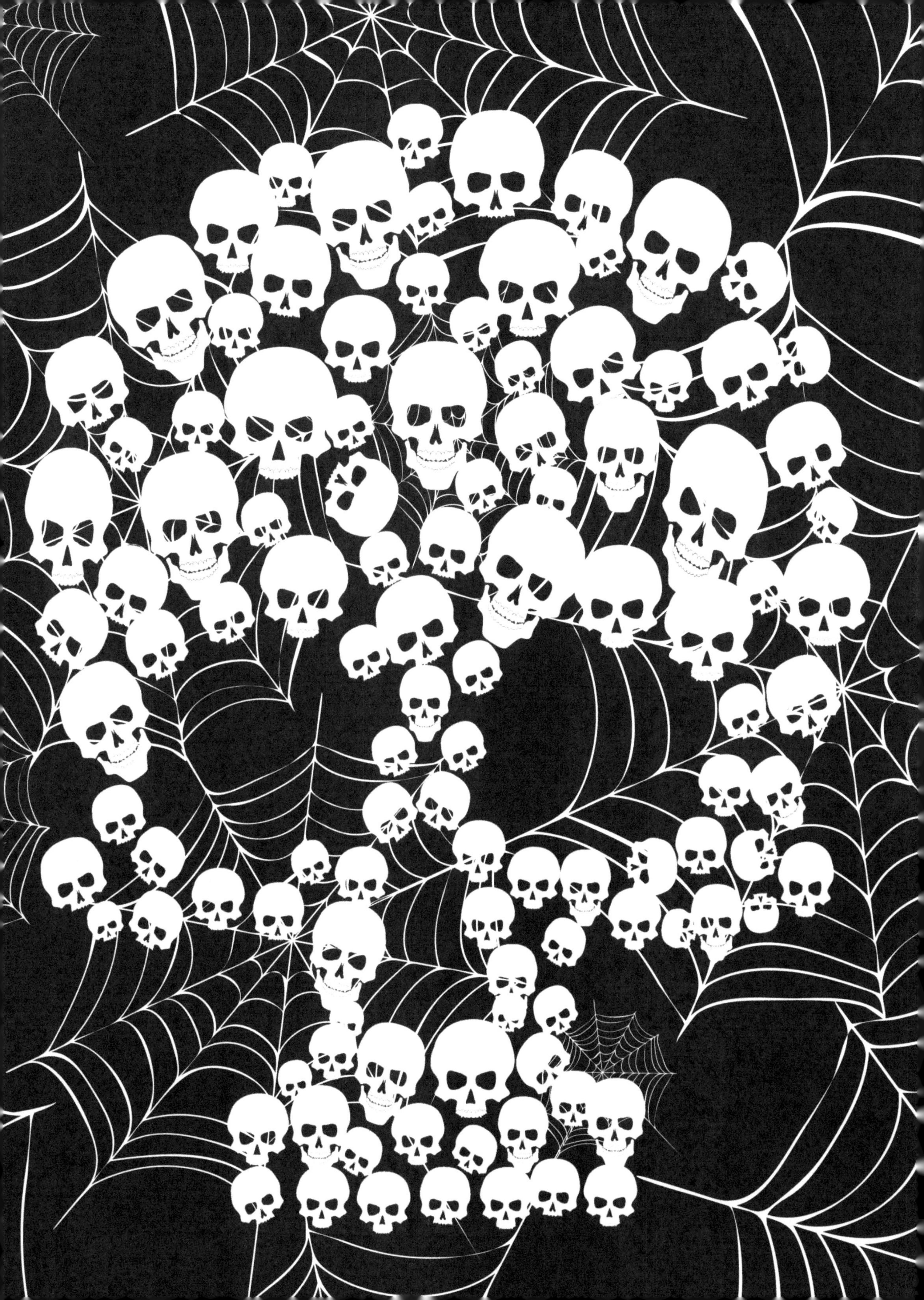

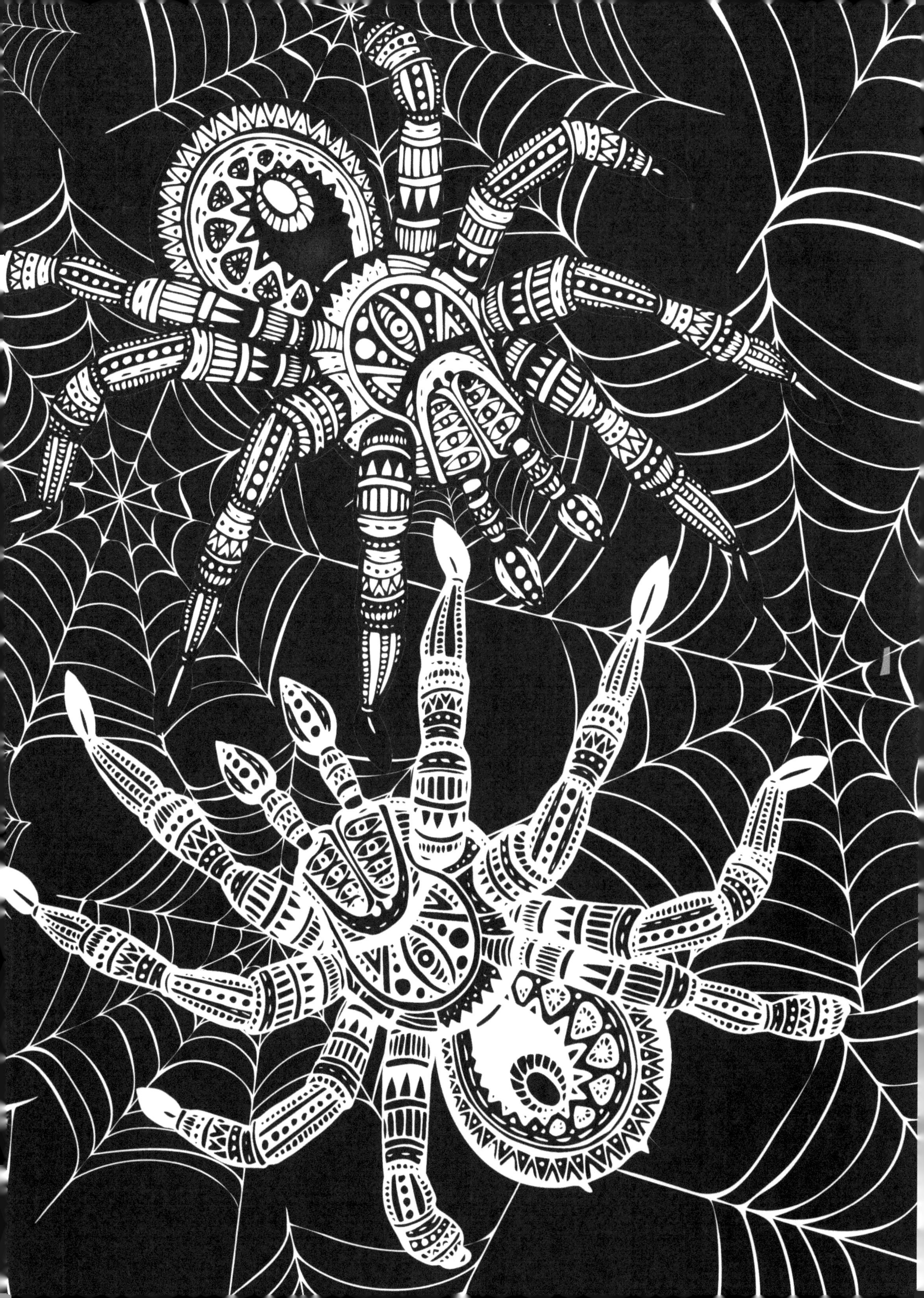

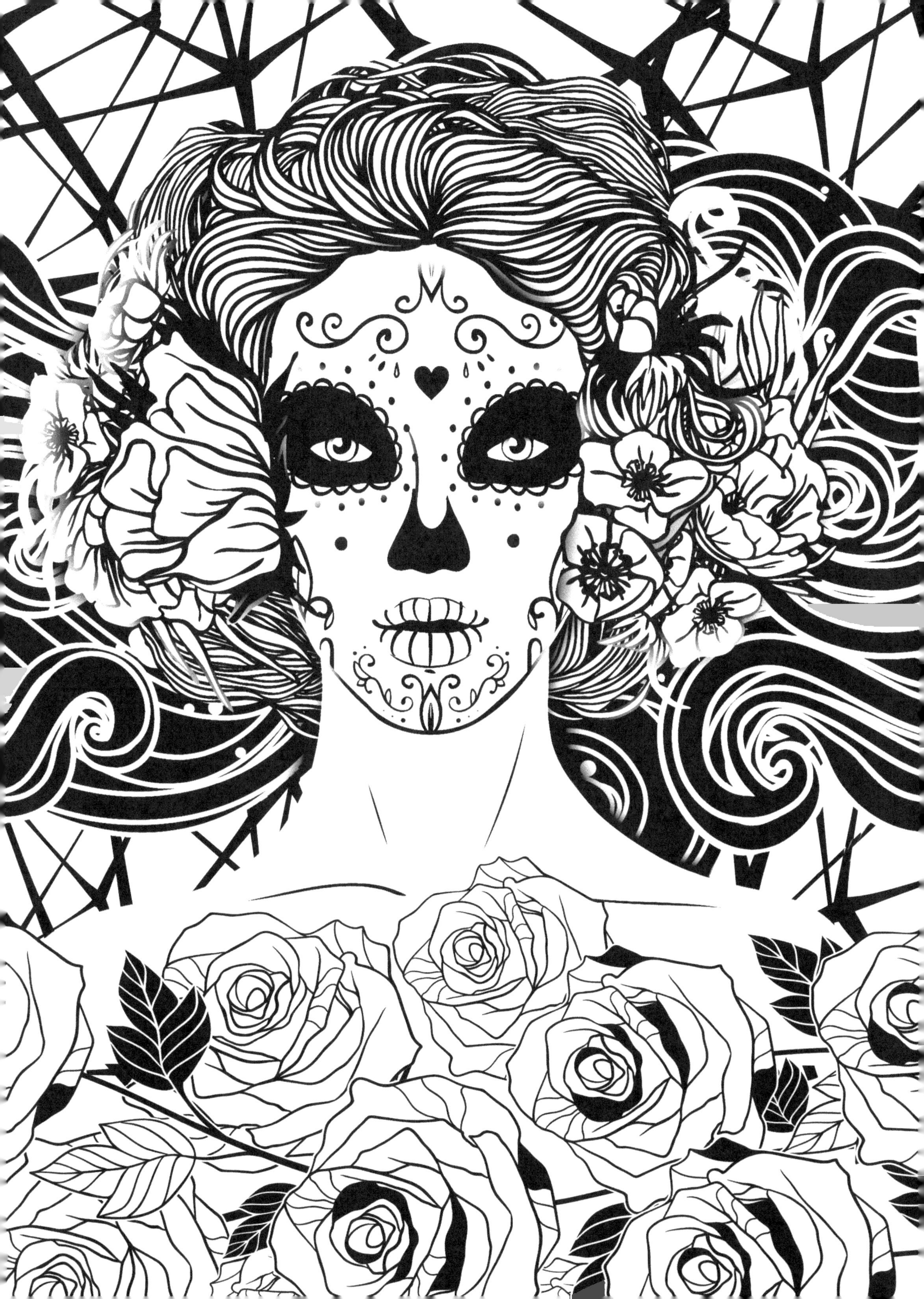

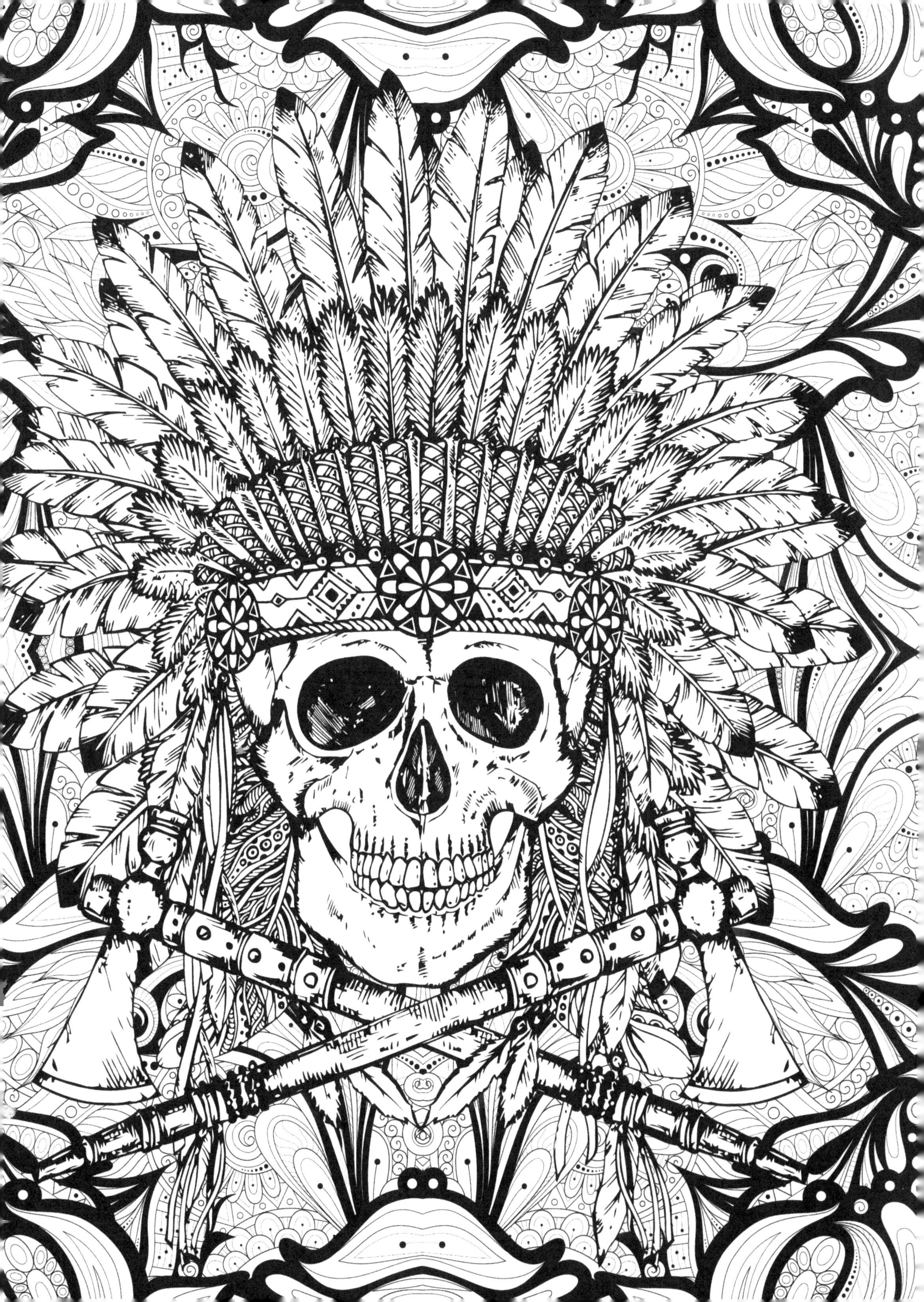

www.ingramcontent.com/pod-product-compliance
Lightning Source LLC
LaVergne TN
LVHW061252100826
845148LV00008B/1107

* 9 7 8 1 6 3 4 1 5 5 4 8 9 *